Politically Incorrect

ISBN: 1 86476 457 0

AXIOM PUBLISHING
www.axiompublishing.com.au
Printed in Malaysia

Politically Incorrect

Words of Mass Deception Exposed

By Michelle O'Regan

Contents

Content Detail

The First Casualty of War
Interrogation Contractors * Perils of Obedience * Groupthink * Terror Speak * Missile Statement * Weapons of Mass Destruction * Mark Twain's Three Kinds of Lies * Assassin * Doublespeak * Why did the chicken cross the road in Iraq? * Waging War—The Boxed set * How to wage War-in-peace * Pre-Emptive Strike... a docudrama.

Politics, Paranoia and Propaganda
What is Politics? * Politics—An Explanation * Terrorist Kit * The Paradigm of Prevention * Children Overboard * How to win elections * Recession? What recession? * Non-core promises * Non-denial denial * Bill and Monica * YMSTBICPC * A Tale of Two Cows * Propaganda * Propaganda techniques * Private Jessica Lynch * The Power of Rhetoric * Political Clichés * Pollitik Speak * Persuasiveness—The tricks of the trade * What a croc!—Behind closed doors.

Political Correctness
What is Political Correctness (PC)? * Modern Lord's Prayer * Ministry of Offensive language * Politically Correct Christmas Holiday Parties * Straight talking vs Politically Correct translation * Politically correct end of year greeting * PC glossary for describing women * PC glossary for describing men * Politically correct cat definitions * A History of Math Lessons * Pees and Queues, Eyes and Tees.

Managers, Their Mission and Mumbo Jumbo
Mission Statements * Ethical Canary * Peter Principle * How many chiefs? * Management speak and what it really means * Employment contract * Job ads decoded * A real job Advertisement * Corporate Irony * A 'Real' Job Application * If Résumés Told the Truth * Answering the tough interview questions * Dear Hiring Manager * Management styles * Tom Swifties of the Workplace * Yuletide CEO announces reforms * Beating meeting blues * Corporate Clichés—A Cynic's Commentary * Evangelising * Employee Benefits—Guidelines * Gobbledygook * Worker dead at desk for 5 days * De-jobbed

Foreword

"Nobody speaks the truth when there's something they must have."

Elizabeth Bowen

We live in an era where many—or is that most—play loose with the truth. Is it because they think we can't handle the truth? That there's no money in telling truth? Or are they so delusional that they actually believe their own rhetoric?

This book is a "scrapbook" of aspects of our lives in the early part of this millennium—a memorabilia of the insane, the inane and the profane—puppetry of the population coming soon to a public arena near you!

They'd have you believe:

- you are being governed by politicians who care, and know how to steer the ship of government without it foundering;
- corporations have a customer service focus;
- managers are empowering their workers to synergise;
- mass media is in the business of balanced reporting or entertainment;
- with this XYZ-thingy your life will be transformed;
- you too can find ever-after happiness with your soul mate by joining the we-take-you-for-a-ride online dating service;
- toxic sludge is good for you;
- you can lose weight as you sleep;
- if you wear this amulet you will have amazing good fortune;
- the opinion gurus and the dispensers of daytime deliverance are in the business because of love not money.

Well is there anyone out there who just wants to shout—

"But the emperor's not wearing any clothes!
He's not making any sense either!
And he's surrounded by bobbleheading yes-men!"

Bamboozlement, insincerity, flummery, trickery, disinformation ...to go!

"Will you have a serve of poppycock with that, on the side?"

The First Casualty of War

"In war, truth is the first casualty."

Aeschylus Greek tragic dramatist (525 BC - 456 BC)

What if somehow we found ourselves in a perpetual state of war—war against terror, war against drugs, war against the latest 'enemy of the state' with all the stage presence of an old horror movie super villain—be it King Kong, or Godzilla or Dracula?

Would truth have to pack its bags and take a very, very long holiday?

For it's not only the lies we are told but it's the self-censorship that prevails when we are told we are at war. "Loose lips sink ships" "You're either for us or you're against us".

Governments and their Oppositions cannot appear to be divided at a time of war. So it's not only the Party line that is toed. It's a silencing of debate effectively on both sides of the house.

It's a time for impassioned rhetoric, fist banging and wild acclaim from the audience. Hearts and minds, hearts and minds.

What of the democratic processes?
Do they pack their possessions, throw them into a handcart and find a hidey-hole, staying clear of 'shellfire' until the *military action* is over?

What of a citizen's right to justice and freedom when there is a prevailing atmosphere of suspicion and paranoia: when the government has a mandate to keep us 'safe' and laws are rushed through so that 'enemies of the state' can be incarcerated, interrogated without trial, imprisoned as 'illegal combatants'?

Indirect terrorism laws are to be implemented in the aftermath of the London 'terrorist attacks'—the authorities must be granted the right to extend their net even further than the 'terrorists' themselves. It must extend to those who 'incite' or 'foment' to acts of terror and whatever else *the small print will denote.*

What are the implications of these proposed new laws and the freedom of expression? Or is that already a misnomer? Did FOE and FOI—Freedom of Expression and Freedom of Information, both die some years ago? Ever since war was declared?

It has been proven that an incumbent leader is very hard to depose in war time. That leader is conferred with 'super powers' giving the impression of strong decisive leadership.

Is it then a coincidence that George W. Bush, Anthony Blair and John Winston Howard were all re-elected with greater majorities?

When a country is in a perpetual state of war, civil laws can be changed radically and expeditiously conferring what amounts to marshall style laws in a democratic state. One can be forgiven for imagining that "1984" that dystopian novel by George Orwell, is compulsory reading for our current *democratic* leaders.

Make no mistake... Truth is MIA... Missing in Action, believed dead.

Interrogation Contractors

"The energy and enthusiasm that our employees bring to the workplace creates an exciting place to work with a constant striving for excellence"

Is this describing the wonderful working conditions of

A theme park?
An ice cream parlour?
Club Med?

No, none of the above.

This is taken from the Titan Corporation's brief—who are they you ask? Only the 'interrogation contractors' for Abu Ghirab and Guatanamo Bay.

"As a member of the Titan team, you will be exposed to the most exciting career adventures situated on the cutting edge of technology".

Perils of Obedience

Stanley Milgram, an experimental scientist at Yale University, set up a simple experiment to test how much pain an ordinary citizen would inflict on another person simply because he was ordered to do so by an authority figure, in this case the scientist.

Person A was strapped into a chair in a booth, an electrode attached to his wrist. Person B is the one at the controls in front of a dialling device that reads: Slight shock, Moderate shock, Strong shock, Very strong shock, Intense shock, Extreme intensity shock, Danger: Severe shock. B is told that he is the 'teacher', his partner in the booth is the 'learner' and the teacher is told that the experiment is about the effect of punishment on learning. B is to read simple word pairs to A, then A is called upon to recall the second word of a pair when he hears the first one. If A makes an error he will have shocks of increasing intensity administered by B.

What Person B does not know is that Person A is not receiving any shocks—A is an actor. Person B is the real focus of the experiment.

As Person A started making mistakes in greater quantity, the authority voice would coldly order Person B to increase the voltage to the mistake-maker. And despite the screams of the subject ringing in his ears, the person at the controls kept obeying the authority voice. It seemed that obedience to stark authority overrode even the highest moral imperatives. There were some who protested but even as they did they kept applying 'electric shocks' to the subject.

"The essence of obedience is that a person comes to view himself as the instrument for carrying out another person's wishes, and he therefore no longer regards himself as responsible for his actions.

Once this critical shift of viewpoint has occurred, all of the essential features of obedience follow. The most far-reaching consequence is that the person feels responsible to the authority directing him but feels no responsibility for the content of the actions that the authority prescribes. Morality does not disappear—it acquires a radically different focus: the subordinate person feels shame or pride depending on how adequately he has performed the actions called for by authority."

The Perils of Obedience By Stanley Milgram

Groupthink

Despite an almost evangelistic promotion of 'teamwork' in the military, politics and management, there is a phenomenon which was identified more than three decades ago that lends a lie to the 'excellence of teamwork'.

Identified by Irving Janis as early as 1972, Groupthink is a concept that refers to flawed decision-making by a group. Groups suffering from this condition desire unanimity at the expense of quality decisions. Highly cohesive groups under extreme pressure to arrive at optimum decisions are most at risk. Janis argued convincingly that the Challenger disaster was a result of the Groupthink phenomenon as was the Bay of Pigs episode in the Kennedy era.

Symptoms of groupthink include:

- Not being critical of each other's ideas
- Not examining other alternatives
- Not seeking expert impartial opinion
- Not having alternative plans
- Deferring to authority figures in the group e.g. CEO or commanding officer
- Being highly selective when gathering evidence i.e. only in support of existing assumptions

Ways to combat the "Groupthink dumb-down" are:

- Including a Devil's Advocate to question all the group's ideas
- Using independent experts
- Separating up the tasks without collusion
- Having a democracy of opinion e.g. that the leaders in the military, politics or bureaucracy leave their authority hats at the door of the meeting, so that others can speak without fear or prejudice.
- Opening up to all possible options, not deriding those that seem less "logical".

Terror Speak

Here are some expressions that were coined because of the "clear and present danger" caused by the War on Terror.

9/11, September 11, 2001
Which has now become a household term, is the date that two airplanes hijacked by terrorists, ploughed into the twin towers in Manhattan.

So September 12
Reminiscent or evocative of the day after the terrorist attacks of September 11, 2001.

Post-traumatic job switcher
Someone who changed jobs because of anxiety or stress caused by the terrorist attacks of 9/11.

Belligerati
Writers and other pundits who prescribe war or manifest destiny.

CNN effect
The negative effect on trade and economics due to the population becoming avid couch potato watching CNN 24/7. "Bringing the war right into your living rooms".

Adrenaline TV
Live TV feed of a dramatic event.

Carnography, Images
Print media or other materials that contain violence or other kinds of carnage.

Weaponise
Attaching a missile or weapon or other 'delivery mechanism'.

Threat fatigue
The kind of weariness that comes from reaching saturation point on constant warnings about 'clear and imminent danger'.

Killology
The study of improved ways of killing humans.

Iraqnophobia
An extreme fear of Iraq and its capacity to manufacture and use biological, chemical and nuclear weapons.

Double-digit midget
A person who's serving in the military and has fewer than 100 days remaining on his tour of duty.

Militainment
News coverage or TV shows and movies about war or the military.

Missile Statement

"We're a company with a proud tradition of first to play our part in making the world a safer place. Our values: to achieve our aim we've established five guiding values, customers our top priority. We will delight all our customers both internal and external by understanding and exceeding all their expectations."

With those feel good words—"delight", "exceeding all their expectations", "proud tradition" one is imagining whipped cream and apple pie, the milk of human kindness maybe. Sorry to disappoint. This is an excerpt from BA Systems' Mission Statement. They make guided missiles.

"Force and fraud are in war the two cardinal virtues."
Thomas Hobbes

Weapons of Mass Destruction

WMDs: Weapons of Mass Destruction
Some expressions travel around the world many times over. They become as familiar a term for us as the names of our own pets, they invade every public and private space, they are writ large on the proverbial wall. This particular acronym of some notoriety is writ larger than most others and will take a very long time to be put to bed in mass memory.

WMDs
Became the chief rationale for invading Iraq and deposing Saddam Hussein. The United Nations opposed the incursion as they felt there was insufficient proof. The weapons inspectors had not uncovered any caches of WMDs. Despite this opposition, the US and its allies invaded on March 21, 2003.

The fact that they found no WMDs, has left rather a lot of egg on the faces of the Allies and led to raising the bar on the level of cynicism experienced by many of the world's citizens.

Here are a few choice quotes to demonstrate how 'absolute unshakeable certainty' can change over time.

"Saddam Hussein's regime is despicable, he is developing weapons of mass destruction, and we cannot leave him doing so unchecked."

Tony Blair, British Prime Minister
10 April 2002

"Iraq has stockpiled biological and chemical weapons, and is rebuilding the facilities used to make more of those weapons. We have sources that tell us that Saddam Hussein recently authorized Iraqi field commanders to use chemical weapons—the very weapons the dictator tells us he does not have."

George W. Bush, US President, 5 October 2002

"We are asked now seriously to accept that in the last few years—contrary to all history, contrary to all intelligence—Saddam decided unilaterally to destroy those weapons. I say that such a claim is palpably absurd."

Tony Blair, British Prime Minister, 18 March 2003

"The Government has decided to commit Australian forces to action to disarm Iraq because we believe it is right, it is lawful and it's in Australia's national interest. We are determined to join other countries to deprive Iraq of its weapons of mass destruction, its chemical and biological weapons, which even in minute quantities are capable of causing death and destruction on a mammoth scale."

John Howard, Australian Prime Minister
Address to the Nation, before the war in Iraq,
20 March 2003

"I never believed that we'd just tumble over weapons of mass destruction in that country."

Donald Rumsfeld, Secretary of Defence, US
4 May 2003

"The premise of the war was... all of the dots added up to a program and to weapons and a weapons program that was dangerous and getting more so."

Dr Condoleezza Rice, National Security Advisor US
September 28, 2003

Mark Twain's Three Kinds of Lies

1) Lies
2) Damned Lies
3) Statistics

Assassin

The CIA had an opening for an assassin. After all of the background checks, interviews, and testing were done there were three finalists: two men and a woman.

For the final test, the CIA agents took one of the men to a large metal door and handed him a gun.
"We must know that you will follow your instructions, no matter what the circumstances. Inside this room, you will find your wife sitting in a chair. Kill her!"

The man said, "You can't be serious. I could never shoot my wife." The agent said, "Then you're not the right man for this job."

The second man was given the same instructions. He took the gun and went into the room. All was quiet for about five minutes.

Then the man came out with tears in his eyes. "I tried, but I can't kill my wife." The agent said, "You don't have what it takes. Take your wife and go home."

Finally, it was the woman's turn. She was given the same instructions to kill her husband. She took the gun and went into the room. Shots were heard, one shot after another. The agents heard screaming, crashing, and banging on the walls. After a few minutes, all was quiet. The door opened slowly and there stood the woman.

She wiped the sweat from her brow, and said, "This gun is loaded with blanks. I had to beat him to death with the chair."

"The world cannot continue to wage war like physical giants and to seek peace like intellectual pygmies"

Basil O'Connor

Doublespeak

What is Doublespeak? It's a language most commonly associated with the military, governments and corporations, a language designed to disguise or distort actual meaning. It can take the form of euphemism e.g. 'decruiting' for firing employees or deliberately ambiguous phrases—"wet work" for assassination.

The term is derived from George Orwell's classic *1984* where Doublethink was the capacity to hold two opposing ideas in one's mind, and Newspeak was the language that arose from the ability to Doublethink.

Doublespeak can have all or some of these attributes:

- Reshapes the unpleasant into something attractive or tolerable
- Creates a false map of the world
- Limits and corrupts thought
- Avoids responsibility through use of passive language
- Makes negative seem positive
- Pretends to be communicating

Nazi doublespeak

The Nazi regime set the bar for coining phrases to hide the truth of their intentions.

Final solution
Extermination of the Jewish people and other 'undesirables'.

Joy Division
Attractive women who were chosen to act as whores for the German soldiers, much as the "comfort women" were selected for the Japanese.

Selection
Under the guise of expert medical determination, the people who came in to the camps were divided into who should live and who should die.

Special treatment of POWs
Meant killing.

Protective custody
Concentration camp.

Duty labour
Slave labour.

Take a firm attitude or take positive measures,
Act with unbridled savagery.

Vietnam War

And the Vietnam War brought its own terms to bear. Here's a sample of the coinages.

Collateral damage
Killing civilians.

Removal with extreme prejudice
Assassination.

Energetic disassembly
Nuclear explosion.

Limited duration protection reaction air strikes
Bombing villages.

Incontinent ordnance
Bombs hitting schools and hospitals by mistake.

Active defence
Invasion.

Today's doublespeak

But now we have progressed into a veritable mushroom strewn field of "military speak" where truth is definitely MIA (Missing in Action) Here are some of the terms used.

Abuse
Torture and humiliation.

Aerial ordnance
Missiles and bombs.

Ally
Not exactly a level playing field, the 'ally' is a fief, a vassal state owing allegiance to the mightier overlord.

Asymmetric warfare
This hardly qualifies as warfare. This is where the gnat takes on the water buffalo and because they are so unevenly matched, the gnat must resort to a whole bag of cunning tricks to irritate and dicomfort the 'enemy' to even make him aware of the nuisance's presence. When little old David continues to fight 'Goliath' that's when the military pundits call it 'asymmetric warfare'. Examples are urban guerilla attacks, the 911 attacks, land mines and suicide bombers.

Axis of Evil
Here's a list of the countries marked as targets for attack and invasion, thus they must be cast as evil. The latest on the US list are Iran, North Korea and now Syria.

Blowback
1) A covert term originally used by the CIA it alluded to the unforeseen consequences of secret American interventions.
2) where there's a threat the American weapons can be turned against them.

Boomerang effect
As in the second meaning of blowback, one's own weapons being used against oneself.

Casualty
This passive term is a euphemism for a person killed or wounded in warfare.

Classified
In World War II there were layers of clearance needed in order to be able to view sensitive documents. In the UK it went restricted, classified, secret etc. so 'classified' was the second lowest in the chain.

Coalition of the willing
Yes well hardly willing! More the allies who can be paid, coerced or bullied into forming part of the 'coalition'.

Coalition of the billing
As happened when the US were seeking approval and allies for invading Iraq, they were not above bribing or making economic threats against countries who don't have much international clout.

Collateral damage
Such a seemingly innocuous sounding phrase that is really covering a multitude, it covers the killing of civilians, environmental contamination by military exercises e.g. the use of Napalm and Agent Orange in the Vietnam war and their effect on the vegetation, and ecological destruction.

Communication
The use of this term has brought it into disrepute—what it really means is propaganda.

Communist
The Cold War's equivalent to what 'terrorist' is to our world since 9/11. The 'commie' was any person or government or individual who opposed the American economic supremacy globally.

Criminal extremist organization
This is a label reserved for anyone posing a perceived threat, steeping in subjectivity of course, they're not telling you how to feel about these 'enemies'!

Crusade
War, but couched in a way to make it sound heroic.
It has been pointed out that the Crusades of the Middle Ages were the Jihad for the young Christian knights. They were assured that if they fought and died in the Crusades their souls would surely go to Heaven, where all kinds of enticements would await.

Decapitation strike
Recently used to describe targeted bombing of structures where it is believed there are political or military leaders.

Defence
This is what it's called when we are justifying being at war. Hard to credit when another sovereignty has been invaded. How can it be legitimately called 'defence'?

Dehousing
World War II—oh yes they had already started with the euphemisms back then—this was the code for the allies bombing raids on German civilian homes.

Detainee
Prisoner of war but not necessarily a 'hot war'. It could be the War On Terror which rages all the time, everywhere.

Disarmament
More commonly involves a coercive arrangement where one side hands over its arms to the other side. But can refer to a mutual agreement for both sides to reduce arms.

Embedded
This was and is a practice by the US military to invite journalists to war, often dressed as soldiers. The catch being that they are censured in what they see, restricted in who they talk to and what they write.

Enemy Combatant
A little verbal segue to get around the Geneva Convention's rights for those captured in combat.

Ethnic cleansing
A euphemism for genocide.

Extraordinary rendition
This is a way of delivering up terror suspects to foreign intelligence services without having to comply with extradition proceedings.

Freedom fighter
A term given to someone fighting on the 'right side'.

Free fire zone
A darling little expression for a free-for-all on bombing villages, journalists, women and children with impunity.

Friendly fire
Not good for morale amongst the troops! This is when they make a major cock up and shoot their own, thus 'friendly'.

Forced disarmament
Just another phrase for war where the small guy is being coerced by the big guy—hardly a fair fight.

Fourth generation warfare
This is supposed to imply that progress is being made, that the war is moving towards some desirable outcome, for one side, anyway.

Illegal combatants
These brethren are truly beyond the pale. They are prisoners of war, stripped of basic human rights and have no right to appeal at the international level either.

Improvised explosive device (IED)
This derogatory term implies the amateurishness of the enemy. Car bombs and such which can not be predicted are given this label.

Intelligence
In military terms it means spying.

Interrogation techniques/methods
Let's not mince words. These are tortures.

Irregulars
This is military speak for "everybody else" not in the know.

Liberate
Yes well not from the viewpoint of the 'liberated' it feels more like invasion, destruction and taking what doesn't belong to them.

Manifest destiny
A pseudo heroic way of describing the inevitable creep of imperialism.

Neutralise
There are more ways than one to neutralise one's enemies—you can kill them, imprison them and strip them of their rights, you can damage their reputation.

Non lethal weapons
It's a toss of the coin whether you die or not from the weapon being used on you.

Patriotism
An unswerving loyalty to one's country, where one must follow whither the powers that be chosen to go, with unbridled zealousness.

Person of interest
Crime suspect.

Pre-dawn vertical insertion
No, not the insertion of a suppository for haemorrhoids! It's an early morning paradrop of troops and equipment as was effected in Granada.

Pre-emptive strike, a fancy term for making an unprovoked attack, also used to provide distraction before the truth is exposed, if ever. "Shoot now, ask questions later" mentality.

Pre-hostility
This is planning for war by making weapons etc. even before hostilities have been initiated.

Propaganda
If this term is used by the military then it means that they are not controlling the message from the opposing side or the independent source.

Regime change
Just another term for a coup, the forceful change of government by a foreign power.

Rendition
Without having any respect for international laws, the deportation of prisoners for the purpose of torture.

Rogue nation
Notice how unashamedly subjective this labelling is! This is another term for the enemy who are not aligned with any other group who will follow the rules of war.

SIEV
Suspected illegal entry vessel. SIEV 4 was the "children overboard" boat.

Servicing the target
An innocuous sounding term which is really about killing the 'enemy' or destroying targeted facilities.

Shaping the battlefield
Doing some early bombing and mayhem work which in turn makes it easier to kill or capture others. This can be achieved by bombarding or shelling targeted areas, before striking.

Shock and awe
This is the term for a massive bombing.

Smart bomb
Bombs configured with guidance systems that can be launched by air and are fairly good at finding their intended targets.

Softening
When they want to go in for a full-scale attack they must first soften the territory eliminating all impediments.

Surgical strike
Insinuates a healing being delivered by the attackers as if they are exorcising a tumour or cancer, and doing it with precision so that no good tissue is removed.

Take down
A euphemism for killing or assassination.

Take out
Destroying a target or assassinating an individual.

Target of Opportunity
The poor misfortunate who has been singled out for assassination; or a target or prey who is encountered or discovered quite by chance.

Terminate with extreme prejudice
Yes it doesn't get any more prejudiced than this, they mean to kill you. And besides 'dead men don't tell tales'.

Terrorists
'If you're not for us you're against us'. All those against American interests are 'terrorists', a very subjective term.

Transfer tubes
A phrase to disguise the body bag the corpses come home in.

Vertically deployed anti-personnel devices
Just a very long-winded way of saying bombs.

Wet work
Not cleaning the shower or bathing the dog, this is assassination a lá Mafia and Military.

Why did the chicken cross the road in Iraq?

Coalition Provisional Authority
The fact that the Iraqi chicken crossed the road affirmatively demonstrates that decision-making authority has been transferred to the chicken well in advance of the scheduled June 30th transition of power. From now on the chicken is responsible for its own decisions.

Halliburton
We were asked to help the chicken cross the road. Given the inherent risk of road crossing and the rarity of chickens, this operation will only cost the US government $326,004.

Muqtada al-Sadr
The chicken was a tool of the evil Coalition and will be killed.

US Army Military Police
We were directed to prepare the chicken to cross the road. As part of these preparations, individual soldiers ran over the chicken repeatedly and then plucked the chicken. We deeply regret the occurrence of any chicken rights violations.

Peshmerga
The chicken crossed the road, and will continue to cross the road, to show its independence and to transport the weapons it needs to defend itself. However, in future, to avoid problems, the chicken will be called a duck, and will wear a plastic bill.

1st Cav
The chicken was not authorized to cross the road without displaying two forms of picture identification. Thus, the chicken was appropriately detained and searched in accordance with current SOPs. We apologize for any embarrassment to the chicken.

As a result of this unfortunate incident, the command has instituted a gender sensitivity training program and all future chicken searches will be conducted by female soldiers.

Al Jazeera
The chicken was forced to cross the road multiple times at gunpoint by a large group of occupation soldiers, according to eye-witnesses. The chicken was then fired upon intentionally in yet another example of the abuse of innocent Iraqi chickens.

Blackwater
We cannot confirm any involvement in the chicken-road-crossing incident.

Translators
Chicken he cross street because bad she tangle regulation. Future chicken table against my request.

U.S. Marine Corps
The chicken is dead.

Waging War—The Boxed set

Hollywood is thinking of taking up the options on a series of movie sequels rivalling Lord of the Rings, Star Wars and Harry Potter for box office blockbuster status. The proposed sequels are:

- WWI—the war to end all wars.
- WWII—a hell of a war!
- Vietnam War—the war you couldn't win.
- Cold War—ideological warfare, the KGB and the CIA.
- War-in-Peace—the war on terror.

How to wage War-in-peace

Compulsory reading list for waging the new War-In-Peace
NOTE: the titles quoted are works of pure fiction. Do not search for the books in stores.

Post-Diplomatic Era
By Talkis Cheep

They Can't Handle The Truth
By Rear Admiral Frank Lee Mendacious

Where in the world are they?
By Hans Auf Blix

Alert not alarmed
By General I.M. Misled

The paradigm of prevention: *Pre-emptive is Always Better*
By Bogus Claims

Man bites dogs of war
By Professor Von Crappshooter

How to create super villains
A Hollywood Handbook for the Military
By Boris Karlough

Make no mistake... Leave that to me!
By G. Dubya

Soundtrack for seamless invasion
Songs to Motivate the Troops
By Hiphop Bodacious

Pre-Emptive Strike... a docudrama

Australia

Howard warns of possible pre-emptive anti-terror strikes – 2/12/2002

"Australia's relationship with Asia, has grown more complicated, after comments by Australian Prime Minister, John Howard, that he'd be prepared to launch a pre-emptive strike in such a case. The Philippines and Thailand have voiced concern... as has Indonesia. The Jakarta Post is reporting an Indonesian Government warning to Australia not to flout international law and rejected any suggestion that Australia has the right to take military action in other countries."

Marginal Candidate: Thank you for coming, Prime Minister. I know how busy you are but these personal appearances do impress people, it can be a great help.

Prime Minister: Delighted to do what I can to help, Alex. How's the campaign going, do you think?

MC: Pretty well, on the whole. I think I can be quietly confident. Without being complacent, of course.

PM: I meant nationally.

MC: Yes, of course, I mean, when I said I, I think I can be quietly confident that the government as a whole will be returned.

PM: I would certainly hope so. I would hope that the Australian people would have the good sense to vote for the people who have made the business of making Australia stronger their top priority. Security, that's the issue.

MC: Quite. We must emphasise the need to be alert but not alarmed.

PM: Nonsense. We've got to scare the living daylights out of them. They're all going to have to vote in a fortnight.

MC: Oh, I am very aware of that. I do wonder though, if there is a danger in perhaps over-emphasising this security angle. "It is, as some of the feedback from my constituents suggests, that aspects of that policy are making them feel more alarmed, than alert."

PM: Such as?

MC: Well, I don't want to exaggerate this, but this pre-emptive strike policy, all this talk of Flying Squads, is making some of my constituents nervous.

PM: My government will put the interests of Australia first. I make no apology for that.

MC: And quite right, too, Prime Minister. I think what some of the voters are worried about is who we have in mind as a target.

PM: Well, we do have someone in mind, but we are not going to tell them, are we?

MC: Obviously not, but a lot of people are worried that we might attack Indonesia.

PM: The trouble with invading Indonesia is you wouldn't know most of the time if you were shooting Muslims or Christians, and I don't think the punters would be happy invading a country run by a military guy called Bang-Bang.

MC: So who do we have in mind as a target? Just privately, of course, between ourselves, Prime Minister.

PM: Think of a country that has brazenly exposed and prosecuted Israeli secret agents? Agents with direct links with Australia.

MC: Not New Zealand?

PM: Exactly. Any attack on Israeli agents is an attack on America's intelligence on the Middle East.

MC: Surely we wouldn't attack New Zealand?

PM: Think weapons of mass destruction.

MC: The All-Blacks?

PM: No, no. They're not that good.

MC: But New Zealand doesn't have WMDs—does it?

PM: Precisely. Not only do they not have them, they do not want them. They have a long history of being actively opposed to nuclear weapons for a start. Name one big American base in New Zealand.

MC: I can't.

PM: Doesn't that worry you? If they are not for us, they are against us. The amount they spend on defence each year is pathetic. New Zealand is the weak link in the Christian Capitalist Alliance in the Pacific region.

MC: Yes, I would agree with that, but—

PM: Take those wogs and foreigners we shipped off to detention camps in Nauru and places. Look how many New Zealand took in as refugees, saying come on in, stay as long as you like. That undermines our tough stance on these queue jumpers.

MC: But what about all the Kiwis living in Australia?

PM: Yes, there is no doubt we have been extensively infiltrated already, but that only makes the need for action more urgent.

MC: What do the Americans think?

PM: Oh, they are all for it. George says he will send Rumsfeld over to give us a hand just as soon as he gets re-elected on November 2.

MC: Well, that's OK, then.

PM: But don't tell that Clarke woman. We want it to be a big surprise.

"Every war when it comes,
or before it comes,
is represented not as a war
but as an act of self-defence
against a homicidal maniac."

George Orwell

"If liberty means anything at all,
it means the right to tell people
what they do not want to hear."

George Orwell

"If the only tool you have is a hammer,
You tend to see every problem
as a nail."

Abraham Maslow

Politics, Paranoia and Propaganda

"Political language—and with variations this is true of all political parties, from Conservatives to Anarchists—is designed to make lies sound truthful and murder respectable, and to give an appearance of solidity to pure wind"

Politics and the English Language
George Orwell

"Giving money and power to government is like giving whiskey and car keys to teenage boys"

P.J. O'Rourke

What is Politics?

Politics is the art of *seeming to appear* to be all things to all men and women. The best indicator of the power of politics to persuade and mesmerize is at election time.

How is it possible to make promises to satisfy the old, the young, the worker, the employer, the family, and the singles? Santa with his goody bag of tax cuts; pension increases; concessions for students; better roads, schools and jobs for all!

Well of course it's a different matter once the Election has been decided—that's the time for promise sorting, the proverbial wheat from the chaff, the core from the non-core.

But what a triumph for the *gullibility fill* and the perpetual appeal of hearing what we want to hear!

Because it doesn't matter how many times our politicians disappoint and renege on their promises, if the electorate were a child and the party in power were the parent, the poor child would be removed by the State and put in care due to malicious neglect and chronic unreliability.

Even if you think you are above politics you can't avoid it. Political influence is endemic, its fetid breath all over us like a hallitosis sufferer's proximity. It touches up against us like the cobwebs in an Indiana Jones epic... like the swarms of creepy crawlies underfoot. You can't run... or you might be shot in the back... you can't hide... you might be dobbed in by a neighbour as a terrorist. You can't use language that may suggest you are discussing political issues in an open manner... "keywords" are being watched and you could be under surveillance by covert government groups as we speak.

Read on if you dare!

Politics – An Explanation

Lil' Johnny goes to his dad and asks, "What is politics?"

Dad says, "Well son, let me try to explain it this way. I'm the breadwinner of the family, so let's call me Capitalism. Mummy is the administrator of the money, so we'll call her the Government. We're here to take care of your needs, so we'll call you The People. The nanny, well, consider her The Working Class. Your baby brother, we'll call him The Future. Now go think about this and see if it makes sense."

So the little boy goes off to bed thinking about what Dad has said. Later that night, he hears his baby brother crying and runs to his room only to find that his diapers are very soiled.

So the little boy goes to his parents' room. Mum is sound asleep. Not wanting to wake her, he goes to the nanny's room. Finding the door locked, he looks through the peephole and sees his father in bed with the nanny. He gives up and goes back to bed.

The next morning, the little boy says to his father, "Dad, I think I understand what politics is now."

"Good son, tell me in your own words then what politics are."

The little boy replies, "Well, while Capitalism is screwing the Working Class, the Government is sound asleep, the People are being ignored and the Future is in deep shit."

If we divine a discrepancy between a man's words and his character, the whole impression of him becomes broken and painful; he revolts the imagination by his lack of unity, and even the good in him is hardly accepted.

Human Nature and the Social Order
Charles Horton Cooley

Terrorist Kit

A "Terrorist Kit" with a letter from the Prime Minister, fridge magnet and some emergency contact numbers as well as a confronting pamphlet detailing how to spot a terrorist and survive an attack, was sent to every Australian household in February 2003, the mail out and the supporting TV ads cost $15 million dollars.

The launch of this material was timed to coincide with President George W. Bush's announcement about invading Iraq.

Many Australians were, unimpressed by this government initiative funded by the taxpayer's dollar and demonstrated their disapproval by returning the fridge magnets in droves.

The Paradigm Of Prevention

"Under the paradigm of prevention, instead of holding people accountable for what you can prove that they have done in the past, you lock them up based on what you think or speculate they might do in the future.

And how can a person who's locked up based on what you think they might do in the future disprove your speculation? It's impossible, and so what ends up happening is the government short-circuits all the processes that are designed to distinguish the innocent from the guilty because they simply don't fit this mode of locking people up for what they might do in the future."

David Cole,
The Power of Nightmares, BBC Documentary

"Facing clear evidence of peril, we cannot wait for the final proof—the smoking gun—that could come in the form of a mushroom cloud."

George W. Bush did not say Hussein was an imminent threat, only that he needed to be stopped before he became a threat.

Children Overboard

"We want to assert the very principle that truth is absolute, truth is supreme, truth is never disposable in national political life."

John Howard,
Australian Prime Minister
25th August 1995

The "children overboard" incident remains an abiding scandal in the annals of Australian Politics. Only weeks before the Federal polling day, November 10, 2001, John Howard, the incumbent Prime Minister, and other spokesmen of the Liberal Party, blatantly used this unsupported rumour that asylum seekers had thrown their children overboard as a way to sway the hearts and minds of the electorate.

The Liberal Party was using Border Protection as a central policy plank, evidenced by the fortune they spent on advertisements, posters and the press.

The "children overboard" was deliberately exaggerated in order to demonise asylum seekers. They were playing on the public's deep-seated fear of a wave of illegal immigrants flooding Australia's shores. Navy and coastal patrol vessels aggressively turned back refugee boats in contravention of their obligations to provide aid under international law.

Here's an example of how a very emotionally charged 'incident', where the emotions being elicited are fear and paranoia and disgust, can prove an election winner for the party prepared to use these tactics.

"I express my anger at the behaviour of those people and I repeat it. I can't comprehend how genuine refugees would throw their children overboard."

John Howard, Australian Prime Minister
Election Campaign, 8th October 2001

Responding to reports that asylum seekers from the vessel SIEV 4 threw their children overboard.

"I do not want people like that in Australia."

John Howard,
Australian National Election Campaign,
October 2001

"They're not the types of people we want integrated in our community"

Alexander Downer,
Minister for Foreign Affairs,
October 2001

How to win elections

"Nothing is more despicable than a professional talker who uses his words as a quack uses his remedies."

Letter to the French Academy, 1714
Francoise de Fenelon

A compulsory reference reading for leaders of democratic nations everywhere.

The Dummies Guide To Winning Elections
By Dr Phellonius Spin

How Paranoia can get you over the line
By D.V.S. Sheister

Xenophobia – Please Explain
By Paul Lini Hansun

Rumours, Allusions and Insinuations
Assistance in Election Season
By Arabella Rumourmonger

Feel the fear and fear it away
By Dr Mesmer Ick

Core and Non-core promises
By Ruprecht Doublspeek

Greenspan-esque

"Since I've become a central banker, I've learned to mumble with great coherence. If I seem unduly clear to you, you must have misunderstood what I said."

Alan Greenspan
Address to the U.S. Congress (1987), quoted in The San Francisco Chronicle, June 9, 1995

Recession? What recession?

"NO... Australia is NOT going into recession!"

Federal Treasurer,
Paul Keating, November 1989

"This is the recession that Australia had to have."

Federal Treasurer,
Paul Keating, January, 1990

Non-core promises

"When I promised "delivery of insulin"...that was a non-core promise..."

John Howard, Australian Prime Minister
Post-election mode.

We, the People, suspected all along that there was some rationale for governments not following through on their election promises.

Non-denial denial

This is the name given to a particular kind of equivocation, basically, it's an apparent denial that although it appeared to be clear-cut and non-ambiguous when it was first heard, on further scrutiny turns out to be no denial at all. It is particularly the preserve of politics and means "Something made to sound like a denial without really being one".

A classic example of this non-denial denial is the then President Clinton's statement about his association with Monica Lewinsky.

"I did not have sexual relations with that woman."

It all hinged as it transpired on his own particular definition of sexual relations which for him meant genital contact. Oral sex or fellatio did not for him qualify as having sex. However to the public he was denying that any sex whatever had taken place.

Bill and Monica

Bill Clinton, 42nd President of the United States, became the first American President since Andrew Johnson to be impeached and tried. Here are some classic Clintonisms.

"It depends on what the meaning of the word 'is' is."

"It depends on how you define alone..."

"There were a lot of times when we were alone,
but I never really thought we were."

-Bill Clinton,
during his 1998 grand jury testimony on the
Monica Lewinsky affair.

YMSTBICPC

"You Might Say That, But I Couldn't Possibly Comment"

This was regularly used by Francis Urquhart (played by Ian Richardson) in the political drama, *House of Cards*, when he wanted to agree with a statement but his hands were effectively tied to agree or disagree publicly. A wonderful finesse to save him from being implicated.

It has remained an acronym in use within the Westminister government and media on occasions when people don't want to commit to a clear Yes.

A Tale of Two Cows

Government regimes and ideologies explained.

British Democracy
You have two cows. Sheep brains is what you put on their feed but it makes them go mad. The government does bugger all.

American Republicanism
You have two cows. You tell them they only have two choices. They're either for us or against us. If they are against us, they lose all their right to green grass, they are called names and are declared traitors. So they say they're for us.

European Unionism
You have two cows. The EU develops a quota system that "limits the gas emissions from flatulent cows." You sell your carbon allotment, and dispose of the milk in an unlicenced landfill site.

Australian Democracy
You have two cows. The government tells you that you can't get paid for their milk because at the last election that was a non-core promise. The government tells you their relatives from Cowzakistan threw their calves overboard so "we don't want that type of cow in the country, thank you".

Communism
You have two cows. You are not allowed to own property unless everyone else has the same. The government takes both but gives you the milk.

Socialism
You have two cows. You give one to your neighbour who has no cows.

Nazism
You have two cows. The government takes both, makes you wear a cow insignia on your clothing and sends you to a concentration camp.

Welfare State
You have two cows. You milk them and then give them each other's milk to drink.

Totalitarianism
You have two cows. However they are seized and all records of them ever having existed is destroyed. All milk is banned.

Propaganda

"Propaganda is to democracy what violence is to totalitarianism"

Propaganda can serve to rally people around a cause, working on their 'hearts and minds' to gain legitimacy for the government's latest initiatives, whether it's invasion of another nation, or getting them behind border reform or a tax initiative.

Propaganda techniques

A number of techniques are employed to generate propaganda. They are summarised as follows

Bandwagon
Inevitable-victory appeals are an attempt to persuade the target group to take the desired course of action because "everyone else is doing it".

- Join the crowd: the desire to be on the winning side is a strong one. The impression is given of an irresistible mass movement impossible to resist.
- Inevitable victory: inviting those not yet on the bandwagon to join those who are already on the road to certain victory. Those already "bandwagoned" are reassured that they took the best course of action.

Appeal to fear
Building support by appealing to fear in the general population. This was an element of the WMD propaganda machine.

Appeal to authority
Citing prominent figures to support an idea, argument, or course of action.

Obtain Disapproval
By convincing the target audience that some idea or behaviour is associated with the groups feared, hated or held in contempt, the propagandist attaches negative connotations to the activity.

A version of this was used in the children overboard scandals. "They're not the kind of people (the ones who throw their babies overboard) we allow into our community".

Direct order

"I want you" was the campaign used to recruit for the US army, Uncle Sam pointing at You. By spelling it out that unambiguously the audience is told what to do without any other choices being provided.

Glittering Generalities

Intense emotionally charged words which are closely associated with the highly valued concepts or beliefs such as freedom, love of country, home, courage and honour. These are calling out for a stamp of approval without any appeal to reason. "The concepts of the propagandist are always good, desirable and virtuous". Beware the unbalanced language of hyperbole.

Rationalisation

Vague or pleasant phrases are used to rationalise questionable acts or beliefs. This is where the doublespeak and euphemism is very effective. If you can call a thorn by another name would it seem as thorny?

Deliberate Vagueness

To be all things to all men one must choose terms which maximise vagueness and that is why the higher level concepts are so useful. To talk of "freedom" and "equality" and so on evokes an emotional but different response in every individual who hears these words. The intention of the propagandist is to motivate the audience without spending any time analysing the validity of the message.

Association

Also known as transference, this is the technique of projecting positive or negative qualities be it praise or blame of a person, object or value on to another in order to make the latter either more acceptable or less palatable. It's employed to transfer blame from one party to another. This could be said to have been used in the Osama Bin Laden connection with Saddam Hussein in justifying an attack upon Iraq.

Oversimplification
Generalities are used to provide simple solutions to complex political, economic, social or military problems.

Common Man
The "ordinary Australian", the "bloke in the bush" approach seeks to persuade an audience that this stance represents the common sense approach of the "common man" or "Joe Public". The propagandist uses ordinary language and recognisable symbols e.g. in Australia the Akubra and a broad Aussie accent to give the impression of wholesomeness and "no flies on me" honesty.

Testimonial
These are quotations especially cited to support or reject a given policy, program, action or personality. You can see this technique used in Election mode. The reputation of the expert is exploited. This plays on us requiring expertise to make up our minds about issues and concerns. "Damaging quotations" can be very effective as well. Candidate X, the incumbent made a foot-in-mouth comment and the opposing party are using it in their campaign to saturation point in the press.

Labelling
The purpose of labels such as "illegal combatants", "dole bludgers" and "queue jumpers" is to arouse the audience's prejudices. Designed to appeal to the negative side of the emotional spectrum e.g. intolerance, fear, disdain, contempt, such reporting often focuses on anecdotal evidence.

Scapegoating
Apportioning blame to a group or organisation which isn't really responsible. This was definitely a propaganda technique used by the Nazis. The Jewish people were blamed for communism and capitalism, for intellectualism and for most of the woes of the world.

Virtue words
Peace, happiness, wise leadership, security, freedom, these are all virtue words. The propagandist will seek to attach these to the group, country, movement or person they are promoting.

Private Jessica Lynch

"One of the most stunning pieces of news management ever conceived"

BBC reporter John Kampfner

"The story of Private Jessica Lynch's rescue was one of the most covered story lines during the war in Iraq. The young soldier from West Virginia was held up as an icon of the strength and spirit of the American volunteer soldier. Her rescue mission was called a daring, made-for-Hollywood story. In recent weeks, however, the stories about Lynch's capture, her time spent captive, and her rescue have been questioned. Many claim that the original reports were filled with inaccuracies that benefited the US government by creating positive feelings about the war."

Dante Chinni, US journalist

"The BBC aired a documentary claiming the military's version of the raid was false. The documentary said the Lynch rescue represented "one of the most stunning pieces of news management ever conceived." BBC reporter John Kampfner charged that the Pentagon had fallen under the influence of Hollywood producer Jerry Bruckheimer. He said Bruckheimer convinced the Pentagon to concentrate on "visuals," even at the expense of the actual facts. The BBC documentary asserted that the dramatic raid was actually unnecessary. It said Iraqi doctors tried to turn Lynch over to the Americans two days earlier, but were turned away by gunfire at a checkpoint. It claimed the Americans knew that Iraqi forces had already left the hospital. In this account, U.S. forces came in firing blanks and setting off explosions, just like in an American action movie."

Notra Trulock, June 16, 2003

The Power of Rhetoric

Rhetoric has, in its many shapes and forms, been around for as long as someone had to persuade another to their point of view by the use of language.

It is an appeal either to our logic (logos) our emotions (pathos) or our character or moral fortitude (ethos). The arena of human affairs where it is most obviously used as a tool of persuasion is in politics. US President John Fitzgerald Kennedy on January 20th 1961, in his speech now known as "Ask not what your country can do for you" employs the rhetoric of 'logos', an appeal to our reason.

"So let us begin anew—remembering on both sides that civility is not a sign of weakness, and sincerity is always subject to proof. Let us never negotiate out of fear. But let us never fear to negotiate.

Let both sides explore what problems unite us instead of belabouring those problems which divide us.

Let both sides, for the first time, formulate serious and precise proposals for the inspection and control of arms—and bring the absolute power to destroy other nations under the absolute control of all nations.

Let both sides seek to invoke the wonders of science instead of its terrors. Together let us explore the stars, conquer the deserts, eradicate disease, tap the ocean depths, and encourage the arts and commerce.

Let both sides unite to heed in all corners of the earth the command of Isaiah—to "undo the heavy burdens—and to let the oppressed go free."

And if a beachhead of cooperation may push back the jungle of suspicion, let both sides join in creating a new endeavour, not a new balance of power, but a new world of law, where the strong are just and the weak secure and the peace preserved."

Martin Luther King Jr., the charismatic African American leader who was a tour de force for human rights in the US in the 60s, demonstrated the power of rhetoric in his unforgettable speech, "I have a dream". This form of rhetoric is called 'pathos', an appeal to our emotions.

"And so let freedom ring from the prodigious hilltops of New Hampshire.

Let freedom ring from the mighty mountains of New York.

Let freedom ring from the heightening Alleghenies of Pennsylvania.

Let freedom ring from the snow-capped Rockies of Colorado.

Let freedom ring from the curvaceous slopes of California.

But not only that:

Let freedom ring from Stone Mountain of Georgia.

Let freedom ring from Lookout Mountain of Tennessee.

Let freedom ring from every hill and molehill of Mississippi.

From every mountainside, let freedom ring …

Free at last! Free at last!

Thank God Almighty, we are free at last!"

Winston Churchill, most famous English statesman of the twentieth century, was a powerful orator and employed rhetoric par excellence. Here in his speech to the faithful servants of Truth and Justice Churchill was first addressing the nation as Prime Minister on the BBC on May 19, 1940. Here is an excerpt appealing to 'ethos', our character.

"Arm yourselves, and be ye men of valour, and be in readiness for the conflict; for it is better for us to perish in battle than to look upon the outrage of our nation and our altar."

And again here in his speech to the Parliament on June 18, 1940, when it was reported that France had fallen to the Germans, and many believed England would soon follow.

"Let us therefore brace ourselves to our duties, and so bear ourselves that if the British Empire and Commonwealth last for a thousand years, men will still say, 'This was their finest hour'."

Once again Winston at his most persuasive in his appeal to character, to moral fortitude. This is an excerpt from a speech made on October 1941 when he was addressing his old alma mater at Harrow.

"Never give in—never, never, never, never, in nothing great or small, large or petty, never give in except to convictions of honour and good sense. Never yield to force; never yield to the apparently overwhelming might of the enemy."

Here then are a few exemplary quotes demonstrating the power of the orator who is able to harness the power of rhetoric.

"People might forget what you said.
They may even forget what you did.
But they will never forget how you made them feel."

Carl W Buechner

Political Clichés

"The minute a phrase becomes current, it becomes an apology for not thinking accurately to the end of the sentence."

letter 1917, Ernest Hemingway

What exactly is a cliché? It's a trite, stereotyped expression, idea or practice. The sad thing about the cliché is that it may well have represented yesterday's truth and might have been able to stimulate thought rather than stultify it. The cliché, cleverly placed at the commencement of a speech or in the middle of a sentence, is the equivalent of putting an infusion of Novocaine into the air conditioning system.

"At the end of the day" was voted the most irritating cliché from around the world for 2004.

Think of political clichés as the linguistic equivalent to grandmother's lullaby being the last thing you hear before you waft off into unconsciousness—they are the doped meat thrown to the 'Rottweilers' zealously guarding our subconscious—a way past the

"Alert! Alert! You are now entering
Subliminal Territory!"

So as innocuous as they seem in all their tattered familiarity, their 'tea and scones' feel, don't be fooled! You are about to be manipulated.

Are you better off today than you were four years ago?
At the end of the day...
Big picture
Drugs wreak havoc on the very fibre of our society.
Each vote is like a human voice.
Every vote is precious.
Every vote is sacred.
Every vote counts.
Every vote must be counted.
Finally, I'd like to thank my wife and family who have stood by me every step of the way.
He appeals to the swing voters.
He cares about children and families.
He connects with the soccer mums.
He connects with the voters.
He got out the vote.
He has a clear vision for our future.
He has a hidden agenda.
He has a voter mandate.
He has begun to reconcile with his family.
He has faced this matter with dignity and honour.
He has flip-flopped on this issue.
He has freely admitted his mistake.

He has taken full responsibility for his actions.
He has to get out and press the flesh.
He has to get out the vote.
He has to rally the party faithful.
He has to solidify the base.
He held his own.
He hit a home run.
He just picked up a key endorsement.
He knows what the country needs.
He ran on a strong party platform.
He regrets any pain he may have caused.
He resonated with the voters.
He should be able to carry the state.
He stayed on message.
He understands the voters.
He won't back down to the special interest groups.
He'll bring dignity to the office.
He'll make a difference in people's lives.
He's a candidate for the people.
He's a centrist.
He's a man of character.
He's a man of great moral fibre.
He's a man of integrity.
He's a man of vision.
He's a visionary.
He's a voter advocate.
He's demonstrated real leadership.
He's gaining momentum in the race.
He's going to throw his hat into the ring.
He's good for the country.
He's his own man.
He's in the hip pocket of big business.
He's just to the left of centre.
He's left-leaning.
He's not ready to claim victory yet.
He's not ready to concede defeat yet.
He's out on the campaign trail.

He's running a grassroots campaign.
He's running on his record.
He's the dark horse in this race.
He's willing to stand up to the Washington bureaucrats.
His record on the issues is clear.
I looked at a poll earlier today and it showed a completely different result.
If we do that, then the terrorists win.
If we ignore votes, we ignore democracy.
I'm sure he can rise above this.
In speeches, use the power fist to give your statements confidence and authority.
It was a landslide election.
It's obviously a jubilant atmosphere here at party headquarters.
It's obviously a sombre mood here at party headquarters.
It's still early.
It's time for a change.
It's time for a new beginning.
It's time for real leadership.
It's time to get tough on crime.
It's time to move forward.
It's time to move on.
I've called the senator and offered my congratulations.
I've never believed in polls.
Key precincts have not yet reported.
Let's celebrate our diversity.
Let's take back our streets from the criminals.
Making long pauses in speeches to give statements extra emphasis.
No dream is beyond our reach.
One incident should not tarnish his many years of distinguished public service.
Our children's future is at stake.
Our country is as strong as it's ever been.
Our democracy is at stake.
Our government has been handed a mandate
People will vote with their conscience.
People will vote with their hearts.

Polls don't mean a thing.
Terrorism wreaks havoc on the very fabric of our democracy.
That's a battleground state.
That's another tax-and-spend program.
That's character assassination.
That's the liberal media bias.
That's what this party stands for.
The bill has support on both sides of the aisle.
The fact of the matter is...
The mainstream press has ignored it.
The middle-class deserve a tax cut.
The party rank and file are behind him.
The people of the great state of ______ have spoken.
The polls fail to show who has the momentum.
The race is a virtual dead heat.
The recount must be full, fair, and accurate.
The true test of character is how you handle adversity.
The voice of the voters must be heard.
The voters are tired of all the name-calling.
The voters are tired of negative campaigning.
The voters can identify with him.
The voters know what he stands for.
The world changed forever on September 11th.
There was a lapse in judgement.
There was an error in judgement.
There's been a lot of mud-slinging in this campaign.
There's no smoking gun.
There's still a long way to go in this race.
They engage in partisan politics.
They're just _______-bashing.
They're playing dirty politics.
They're playing political football.
They're running neck and neck.
They're trying to steal the election.
This campaign will focus on the issues.
This country has a proud heritage.
This country has come a long way.

This country is headed in the right direction.
This is a fishing expedition.
This is a private matter that's being dragged through the press.
This is a smear campaign.
This race is too close to call.
Together, we'll build our future.
We all make mistakes.
We are the defenders of freedom around the world.
We can't disenfranchise the voters.
We don't want a fast result, we want an accurate result.
We have a changing political landscape.
We have to look to the future.
We must determine the will of the people.
We must do what's in the best interest of the country.
We must follow the rule of law.
We must let the healing process begin.
We must put children first.
We must put this unfortunate chapter behind us.
We must win the war on drugs.
We need affordable prescription drugs for seniors.
We still have a lot to do.
We'll empower people.
We'll fight for working families.
We'll find out how great a nation we can be.
We'll grow the economy.
We'll leave no child behind.
We'll reach across party lines.
We're a better, stronger country than we were four years ago.
We're all human.
We're expecting a strong voter turnout.
We're going to reform government.
We're headed down a slippery slope.
We're one people bound together by a common set of ideas.
We're the leaders of the free world.
What matters is how people vote on Election Day.
What's happening in the ______ camp?
With all due respect...

You can't change the rules in the middle of the game.
You have to question the timing of this story

Pollitik Speak

Here are a list of coined terms that are able, with their wit and colour, to give a real idea of what politics looks like in modern democracies at the start of this millennium.

Dog-whistle politics
This is the kind of political message that has the same effect as a high pitched dog whistle has on pooches. Ignored or just inaudible to most of Joe Citizens, it is nevertheless heard very clearly by the target audience. The target audience comes to heel and rolls on its belly.

Corpocracy
This describes a society where corporations are the chief executers of both economic and political power.

Democrazy
A democracy which should be certified insane such are the senseless or unjust events it tolerates.

Pollutician
A politician who has no regard for the environmental bottom line and supports initiatives and policies which are known to harm the environment.

Xerocracy
1) This describes a society where censorship is so endemic that the only way to disseminate information is via photocopied documents and newsletters which have been written covertly.
2) The one who photocopies is the one who rules.

Just-in-time politics
Instead of parties or ideologies, this kind of politics is ad hoc and the coalitions form around issues.

Declinism
This is the belief that a country, economic or political system is headed on an inevitable spiral of decline.

Attack Fax
A fax sent to the media maligning the ideas or conduct of the groups rivals or opponents.

Environomics
The kind of fiscal policy or business stratagem relying on overly optimistic economic forecasts and unsustainably high levels of spending.

Headline Risk
A spin doctor's nightmare, the kind of headline that could cause an inordinate amount of negative publicity to the cause whatever it is.

Frontrunneritis
The inclination for a candidate seen to be winning the race to be exposed to a greater degree of scrutiny.

Shift and shaft
The knack government has to devolve programs to a lower level of government without providing any means or a budget to pay for said programs.

Spinnable
Susceptible to the influence of biased or slanted information.

Avoision
The no-man's land grey area of ambiguity that falls between legal avoidance and illegal evasion.

Fiscalamity
Catastrophic economic or financial distress caused by fiscal mismanagement.

Soft power
Power based on the qualitative influences such as values, culture or ideology.

Self-coup
The lightning overthrow of a government by its current leader in a ploy to gain even more power.

Globitarian
The kind of government where all programs and decisions are determined by global market forces.

Persuasiveness
The tricks of the trade

Here you ever wondered what lies at the heart of the hypnotic and manipulative language of the politician, the businessman, the spin doctor? When what passes for communication is so deliberately vague and imprecise that the audience is required to "fill in the gaps" for themselves to give it meaning.

That way you can be all things to all men! And you don't have to worry too much about accountability or responsibility for the things you say and what you promise. Here is an analysis of what they are doing:

- **All-or-nothing thinking**
  Black/white, either/or polarized to the extremes.

  Example: Either you are with us, or you are with the terrorists.

- **Can't-ing**
  By using the 'can't' and the 'cannot' word, the speaker imposes limits on those hearing the message.

  Example: We can't just sit back and hope that diplomacy will work.

  Example: We cannot tolerate non-team players.

- **Circular Reasoning**
  When the reason given is the same as the matter being explained, there is in effect no explanation being offered.

  Example: We are letting staff go because we are not retaining them.

- **Distortion**
  Using words like 'necessary' and 'inevitable' makes a kind of judgement without any of the responsibility. Who evaluates the 'unavoidability'? What are the criteria and standards by which you decide on 'unavoidability'?

  Example: We don't want to kill civilians but in war it's unavoidable.

- **Emotionalising**

  Putting a greater store in emotions than in objective information.

  Example: Our grief and anger will not have any peace until we have hunted them down.

  Example: We have to defend our deeply held values

  Example: Our people are lost and in despair, they are crying out for meaning in their lives!

- **Empty Statements**

  'Communication' that is like chaff.

  Example: The state of high alert is not as critical as it seems.

- **Filtering**

  Putting the spotlight on one thing to the exclusion of everything else.

  Example: We must focus on military solutions = what about diplomacy and negotiations? What happened to peaceful means of solving disputes?

- **I think**

  Don't be fooled by this one. When this is used, add parentheses around the statement. The small print means 'this is the speaker's own opinion and should not reflect negatively on the corporation, the government, the religious institution or the product being flogged'. No undertaking has been made, it is just an opinion.

  Example: I think we could benefit from more women in the military forces.

  Example: The shelling of the village was regrettable, but it was necessary.

- **Labelling**

  To use repetitive name-calling, using dismissive derogatory labels or else emotional trigger words.

  Examples: 'illegals' for refugees who have broken no Australian laws, 'bludgers' for the unemployed, 'terrorist' to describe the enemies of the hour.

- **Mind Reading**
  Assumptions and projections about someone else's thoughts.

  Example: They hate our freedoms. We love things, they hate things.

- **Negative Declarations**
  Stating categorically and forcefully what is NOT the case. By stating what is not the case does not follow that it is telling us what is the case.

  Example: "The Marketing Executive will not be fired". This does not imply that he won't be persuaded to seek other job opportunities.

  Example: "There will be no redundancies". Which does not mean that staff will leave for other reasons as in being managed out or given the 'white wall treatment' or the services being outsourced. There are many names you can call being given the 'shove'.

- **Opposite Qualifiers**
  When there's an inherent contradiction in the description itself.

  Example: "This small matter is in effect not small at all."

- **Over-Generalisation**
  Sweeping statements, the larger the sweep, the wilder the hysteria from the crowd!

  Example: This is the world's fight. This is civilisation's last stand

  Example: Killing is a way of life for these people. They are a truly barbaric culture.

- **Presupposition**
  These are the silent assumptions, the unspoken "if and then" statements. Unless you know more, you are not in a situation to make a judgment.

  Example: If people knew more of the true extent of the terrorist networks, they would not question our right to bring in the anti-terrorist laws.

- **Rhetorical Questions**
  Unanswered questions form a vague outline of things omitted. Often when politicians use this technique they do so to wild and unmitigated applause, but what are they doing about any of it? It presses emotional buttons and that is all.

  Example: When will we be free of terrorism? Will our enemies lay down their arms? When will there be peace and justice for all?

- **Should-ing**
  Statements with "should", "must", "have to" and "need to" put the audience under some pressure to follow a series of rules plucked from 'where?'

  Example: We need to be especially vigilant.

  Example: We should revisit the vision statement and do our utmost to adhere to the corporate values.

What a Croc! – Behind closed doors

Headlines 12 October 2004, BBC newsround

Granny saves man from Crocodile

A 60-year-old grandma has saved a man from a crocodile attack in Queensland by jumping on the back of the creature. Alicia Sorohan dived on top of the saltwater croc when she saw the beast dragging her friend from his tent in northern Australia.

Kicking and poking the 4.2 metre crocodile, the heroic grandma managed to distract it long enough to enable her friend to escape.

The pair were airlifted to hospital and are now recovering from the drama…"

"This – " The Minister for Tourism jabbed her long-nailed finger repeatedly at the newspaper she had tossed on the table in front of her, "this is a ... a ... a ..."

"Catastrophe?"

"Yes, thank you, Robert. This is a catastrophe."

"They'll strangle Medicare?"

"They'll destroy workers' rights?"

"They'll axe environmental research?"

"Primary school fees will multiply?"

"Refugees will be locked up forever?"

"Packer and Murdoch will own everything?"

"American companies will cover the country with genetically modified crops?"

"We'll never get out of Iraq?"

"They'll abolish the Senate?"

"They'll abolish the States?"

"Churchgoing will become compulsory?"

The fingernail, clearly irritated, rapped the table for attention.

"Excuse me, this is supposed to be a crisis meeting on tourism, not a gripe session by a bunch of lefties and greenies. Didn't any of you vote Liberal?"

Silence.

"Humph. Well, some of us obviously know more than others what the people want. But what none of us want ", the fingernail started jabbing the newspaper again "is this sort of thing: 'Gutsy granny grabs killer croc in Queensland camping nightmare'. What do we think this means for tourism?"

"It's a catastrophe?"

"Thank you, Mike. It is a catastrophe. What do you all suggest we do about it?"

"Think Positive."

"It's only for three years."

The fingernail rapped the table sharply. "Focus, focus please! Some of us are not focusing on the issue here. Indeed, I have thought for some time that certain members of this cabinet would benefit greatly from attending a weekend motivational course."

"With respect, Minister, I don't think we should over-react. After all, that Irwin chap has made an absolute fortune out of crocodiles on TV and there is no doubt he has done a tremendous job in raising Australia's profile overseas."

"Perhaps we could get Crocodile Dundee to throw a few more shrimps on the barbie?"

"Linda Kowalski's better-looking, could we get her to cook the shrimps?"

"In a bikini? Spattered with fat?"

"She could wear an apron."

"Yes! With a big croc on the front—"

"Put her in tight shorts with a croc—"

The fingernail jackhammered the table. "I don't believe what I am hearing!... Yes, George?"

"I would suggest we need to be a little careful in deconstructing this crocodile concept. There is undoubtedly an element that appeals to vicarious thrill-seekers"

"You mean, the hint of danger, the adventure?"

"Forget Kowalski! Why don't we hire the granny as tourism ambassador?"

"Wait on, wait on. The croc almost killed her, she nearly had her head bitten off. What sort of message do you think she would give the world? 'If you want to camp on the North Queensland coast, bring a bloody big gun'?"

"That could be a problem for airport security. Not to mention the anti-gun lobby."

"And the wildlife conservation people."

Tap, tap, tap! "Well, George, how would you deconstruct this crocodile thrill paradigm?"

"I think we need to avoid the more gory details. We need to focus on the concept that adventure can be fun."

"You are sound asleep at four in the morning and a huge primeval beast shoves its head into your tent and sinks its fangs into your thigh. Doesn't sound much like fun."

"Sounds like a Japanese game show."

"What about a toy, a mascot, like that fat-arsed wombat we had for the Olympics?"

"We need something special—what about a little green plastic croc with spring-loaded jaws and a swivelling neck so that when you pressed its back the head spins round and bites your finger?"

The fingernail rapped the table authoritatively. "Robert, I think that is an excellent idea. I am sure we would be able to get them made in Asia cheaply enough to be able to give every Queensland tourist one as a free souvenir when they leave. In fact, there is a toys and novelty fair coming up in Jakarta next month. I suggest that Robert and I should perhaps attend that fair as a fact-finding mission. Can you make yourself available for the third weekend of the month, Robert? Good. Now, any other business? Albert?"

"See if you can get little models of Johnny Howard to put on the crocodiles' backs."

Political Correctness

"Political correctness uses the excuse of not hurting anyone, the Politically Correct are demanding that people behave like the fool who would please everyone, whilst everyone must become such a fool!"

Philip Atkinson

"He calls poor people poor, instead of underprivileged,
Claiming that the English language is becoming overdrivileged."

Ogden Nash

I used to think I was poor.
Then they told me I wasn't poor, I was needy.
Then they told me it was self-defeating to think of myself as needy.
I was deprived.
(Oh not deprived but rather underprivileged)
Then they told me that underprivileged was overused.
I was disadvantaged.
I still don't have a dime.
But I have a great vocabulary.

Jules Pfeiffer

What is Political Correctness (PC)?

PC stands for Politically Correct. We of the Politically Correct philosophy believe in increasing a tolerance for a Diversity of cultures, race, gender, ideology and alternate lifestyles. Political Correctness is the only social and morally acceptable outlook. Anyone who disagrees with this philosophy is bigoted, biased, sexist, and/or closed-minded.

Q: **Why should I join your ranks?**
Being PC is fun. PC-ism is not just an attitude, it is a way of life! PC offers the satisfaction of knowing that you are undoing the social evils of centuries of oppression.

Q: I am a white male. Can I still be PC?
Sure. You just have to feel very guilty.

Q: Please explain.
If you are a white male, your ancestors were responsible for practically every injustice in the world—slavery, war, genocide and plaid sports coats. That means that YOU are partially responsible for these atrocities. Now it is time to balance the scales of justice for the descendants of those individuals whose ancestors your ancestors pushed down.

Q: How do I do that?
It's simple. You've got to be careful what you say, what you think, and what you do. You just don't want to offend anyone.

Q: You mean I should guard against offending anyone?
That's right. Being offensive is destructive, and will not make the world a harmonious utopia, like in John Lennon's *Imagine.*

Q: How else can I join in?
Oh, there are lots of ways. For example, why buy regular ice cream when you can buy "Rain Forest Crunch?" Segrega...whoops, separate all of your garbage into different containers: glass, metal, white paper, blue paper, plastic, etc. Make sure that all your make-up has not been tested on animals. Try to find at least sixty ways to use your water; when you take a shower, brush your teeth at the same time. Then don't let the water go down the drain, use it to irrigate your lawn. Or better yet, replace your lawn with a vegetable garden. Don't use aerosol. And by all means, don't burn or deface our flag. Remember, as a citizen of Canada, you're living in God's country.

If you are fortunate enough to know your ethnic heritage, dress the part! Don't do drugs. You should listen to at least one of the following PC musicians: U2, REM, Sinead O'Connor, Sting, or KD Lang.

Harrass people who wear fur coats. Remind them that an innocent baby seal was mercilessly clubbed. Or just yell, "fur." They hate that. And don't ever eat meat.

Q: Not eat meat? That's a bit extreme
Cows are animals, just like humans are animals. That means that they have rights. When you eat meat, you're oppressing animals!

Q: How do I know when an animal has rights?
The general rule is as follows:

If an animal is rare, pretty, big, cute, furry, huggable, or lovable, then it has rights.

Examine the following chart:

Rights	**No Rights**
cows	cockroaches
cute bunnies	flies
dolphins in tuna nets	tuna in tuna nets
whales	sharks
red squirrels	gray squirrels
owls	loggers
harbor seals	barnacles

Q: Wow. What else can I do to be PC?
Hug a tree. Rejoice each day in our cultural differences, for they are what gives flavour to our great country. Get in touch with your sexual identity. Check your refrigerator for freon leaks. Subscribe to National Geographic. Search it for neat non-Western cultural traditions and costumes. After you read it, use the paper as an alternate fuel source.

Q: I don't know about all this.
If you are feeling unsure about your motivation, just remember. You are right. It's that simple. You are right.

Q: How do I know if an action is non-PC?
Good question. It's important to know when someone is saying something insensitive so that you can have that person removed from society. The guideline is as follows:

Is the confrontation between two white people? Yes—The liberal is right. No—The white person is oppressing the ethnic person.

Here's a fun practice drill for you: See how many newspaper articles you can make into race bias stories. It's fun! Some PCers are so good they can make the weather report look like a KKK pamphlet!

Q: What should I do if I see someone doing something Non-PC?
It all depends on the situation. If you are not in a position of authority, by all means report this activity immediately to whomever is in charge. If your school leader, employer, or superior is hip to the trend of the 90s, she or he will take the necessary steps to have the insensitive offender disciplined.

Q: But isn't that censorship?
That's not what free speech is about. Some call it censorship. PCers call it "selective" speech. Saying something negative about a particular race or gender is just as damaging as, say, punching them in the face. We just can't allow that kind of verbal assault.

Q: I've heard a lot about PC words to replace "Black," "Indian." etc.
Yes. That's part of the PC movement. You see, part of the way we think about people comes directly from the words we use to describe them. Take "black" for instance. Why should a person be judged by the colour of their skin?

Q: You mean they should rather be judged by the content of their character?
No, I mean they should be judged by where their ancestors are from. If your great grandparents are from Africa, or Asia, or wherever, then you should be identified by that fact. You can even apply for special scholarships!

Q: I'm a mixture of French, German, English, and Russian. Can I get one?
No, there are none offered to white males however, if you are a woman, oops, womyn, there should be plenty.

Q Hey, wouldn't a white person From Libya or Egypt technically be an African-Canadian?
Technically, yes. But that's not the kind of African-Canadian we mean. That is, we're really talking about skin colour, but we're pretending that we aren't. Another example: A white South African immigrant is not an African-Canadian or either.

Q: How can I learn to make my language more Politically Correct?
For more help, see the PC Lexicon at the end of the handbook. (next issue)

Q: I'd like my child to be PC. What can I do?
Well, for one thing, we should forcibly encourage students to volunteer their time with philanthropies. Also, we should re-emphasize non-Western perspectives on history. Finally, we should re-structure tests and quizzes to reflect cultural biases.

Q: I Don't get it.
Well, the way the system works now, "select" under-represented minorities who tend to do worse on entrance tests have lower standards of admissions at school and work and receive preferential treatment. This is unfair and wrong.

Q: It is?
Yes. The truly PC way to do it is to have a different grading scale for different groups which gives or subtracts points from the final score, depending on who is taking the test. If you are white, then you have been benefited by society during your life. That means that you lose ten to fifteen points to make the test fair to everyone else.

Q: I Guess that sounds right.
It IS right. That's the beauty of PC.

Q: What else do I have to be careful of?
Humour. PC people take every comment very seriously. We will not accept any comment, joke, remark, or anything that sounds like it could be a racial slur.

Q: Give me an example.
"What's black and white and red all over?" has been staple humour for decades. Not PC—it can be taken the wrong way.

In every day speech, try to use phrases like, "Isn't that the pot calling the kettle elegantly dusky." Any racial jokes or jokes even mentioning culture or gender should be omitted. True, this mostly limits comedy to the level of sitcoms, but that's the price you pay for social equality.

Q: Is that all there is to it?
Yes. The Politically Correct belief is essentially recognition that people are diversely equal. We rejoice in this equality by treating people differently based on their equal individuality. Hop aboard the bandwagon. Be PC. Or you're an intolerant, racist, sexist insensitive pig.

Attribution, University of Michigan

Touché

A politically correct reporter's question to a wheelchair occupant?

"What's it like being ambulently challenged?"
"What's it like being euphemistically endowed?"

Modern Lord's Prayer

Our universal chairperson in outer space
your identity enjoys the highest rating on a prioritised selectivity scale may your sphere of influence take on reality parameters
may your mindset be implemented on this planet as in outer space.
Allot to us, at this point in time and on a per diem basis, a sufficient and balanced dietary food intake
and rationalise a disclaimer against our negative feedback
as we rationalise a disclaimer against the negative feedback of others and deprogram our negative potentialities
but desensitise the impact of the counter-productive force
for yours is the dominant sphere of influence
the ultimate capability (non-nuclear)
and the highest qualitative analysis rating
at this point in time and extending beyond a limited time-frame.

Ministry of Offensive language

The ministry, after much consultation with any number of groups, associations, lobby groups, has arrived at the conclusion that there is nothing inherently offensive about any one word, and the business of what constitutes offensive language is a very subjective matter.

However, culture nuances being what they are, there are terms which become offensive because of the manner and context of their use, and common linguistic idiom.

Presently, in the early part of this millennium and with the advent of Political Correctness, it is perceived as important that gender stereotypes are removed from public language.

Here are the guidelines for using gender-neutral expressions.

Sexist references

Man/men having been used repeatedly throughout human discourse to imply mankind must stop as often as is possible, feasible and implementable

Out	In
Mankind	Human beings
Man	Humans
	Humankind
	People
	Society
	Men and women
Man-made	Synthetic
	Artificial
Man in the street	Average person
	Ordinary person

Taking the gender out of occupations

Stereotypes must be eschewed—there are no longer any fields which are now simply the preserve of men or women.

Out	In
Anchorman	Anchor
Bellman, bellboy	Bellhop or bellehop
Businessman	Business person, manager, executive, retailer etc
Chairman, chairwoman	Chair, chaise, or chairperson
Cleaning lady	Housecleaner, housekeeper
Maid	Office cleaner, gofer, cleaning person
Clergyman	Priest, Rabbi, cleric, clerique, member of the clergy

Congressman	Member of congress, Representative
Fireman	Fire fighter or fair fire fighter
Forefather	Ancestor, foreparent
Girl Friday, secretary	Person Friday, assistant, Director of First Impressions
Housewife	Homemaker, domestic engineer
Insurance man	Insurance agent
Layman	Layette, layperson, nonspecialist, nonprofessional
Mailman, postman	Mail or letter carrier or courier
Policeman	Police officer, law enforcement officer
Salesman, saleswoman,	Salesperson, sales representative,
Saleslady, salesgirl	sales associate, clerk
Spokesman	Spokesperson, representative
Stewardess, steward	Flight attendant
Weatherman	Meteorologist, weather reporter, weathercaster
Workman, labourer	Worker
Actress	Actor

'He' must be purged

'He' as a pronoun must be expunged because it can be seen to exclude women, exception being Hebrew where 'he' means 'she' and 'who' means 'he'. Of course the exception to this is when the he, him, himself etc does refer to a he, in which case it is perfectly acceptable.

Out	In
When a driver approaches a red light he must prepare to stop	When drivers approach a red light, they must prepare to stop. Or When approaching a red light, a driver must prepare to stop.

Names, Titles, Descriptions where both sexes mentioned

Consistency is the key, unless there is a special reason for not being so.

Out	In
Dear sir	Dear sir/madam, Dear sir or madam, Dear madam or sir or To whom it may concern
Men and ladies	Men and women, ladies and gentlemen
Betty Schleigelhoosengrott, an attractive 49 year old physician and her husband, Alan Phitzweiler, a noted editor	Betty Schleigelhoosengrott, a physician, and her husband, Alan Phitzweiler, an editor
Mr Peter Piper and Mrs Myrtle Gruber	Mr Peter Piper and Ms Myrtle Gruber (unless you know Mrs is her preference)
Man and wife	Husband and wife

Race, Ethnicity and national origin

Some terms referring to racial and ethnic groups are quite clearly offensive, for example, Oriental, coloured. They can be outmoded or inaccurate. For example, Hispanic is a generic term for Spanish-speaking people of the Western Hemisphere but if possible use the more specific term e.g. Mexican/American or Latino.

"Political correctness allows for
two basic
types of complaint:
that people who behave the same
are treated differently,
and that people who behave differently
are treated the same"

Anon

Politically Correct proverbs

See if you can work out these familiar proverbs in amongst all the delicacy of language. If you can you may be a born decipherer of BS.

1. Pulchritude possesses solely cutaneous profundity.
2. Scintillate, scintillate asteroid minific.
3. Members of an avian species of identical plumage congregate.
4. Surveillance should precede saltitation.
5. It is fruitless to become lachrymose over precipitately departed lacteal fluid.
6. Freedom from incrustrations of grime is contiguous to divinity.
7. The stylus is more potent than the claymore.
8. It is fruitless to indoctrinate a super-annuated canine with innovative manoeuvres.
9. Eschew the implement of corrections and vitiate the scion.
10. The temperature of the aqueous content of an unremittingly ogled cooking container does not reach 212 degrees Fahrenheit.
11. Neophyte's serendipity.
12. Male cadavers are incapable of yielding testimony.

13. Individuals who make their abode in vitreous edifices would be advised to refrain from catapulting petrous projectiles.
14. All articles that coruscate with resplendence are not truly auriferous.
15. Where there are visible vapours having their province in ignited carbonaceous material, there is conflagration.
16. Sorting on the part of mendicants must be interdicted.
17. A plethora of individuals with expertise in culinary techniques vitiates the potable concoction produced by steeping comestibles.
18. Exclusive dedication to necessary chores without interludes of hedonistic diversion renders John a heptudinous fellow.
19. A revolving lathic conglomerate accumulates no diminutive claucous bryphitic plants.
20. The person presenting the ultimate cachinnation possesses, thereby, the optimal cachinnation.
21. Missiles of ligneous or porous consistency have the potential of fracturing my osseous structure, but appellations will eternally be benign.

Politically Correct Christmas Holiday Parties

FROM: Patty Lewis, Human Resources Director
TO: All Employees
RE: Christmas Party
DATE: December 1

I'm happy to inform you that the company Christmas Party will take place on December 23, starting at noon in the banquet room at Luigi's Open Pit Barbecue. No-host bar, but plenty of eggnog! We'll have a small band playing traditional carols, feel free to sing along. And don't be surprised if our CEO shows up dressed as Santa Claus! A Christmas tree will be lit at 1:00 P.M. Exchange of gifts among employees can be done at that time, however, no gift should be over $10.00 to make the giving of gifts easy for everyone's pockets. This gathering is only for employees! A special announcement will be made by our CEO at that time!
Merry Christmas to you and your family.

FROM: Patty Lewis, Human Resources Director
TO: All Employees
RE: Holiday Party
DATE: December 2

In no way was yesterday's memo intended to exclude our Jewish employees. We recognize that Chanukah is an important holiday which often coincides with Christmas, though unfortunately not this year. However, from now on we're calling it our "Holiday Party". The same policy applies to employees who are celebrating Kwanzaa at this time. There will be no Christmas tree present. No, Christmas carols sung. We will have other types of music for your enjoyment. Happy now?
Happy Holidays to you and your family.

Patty

FROM: Patty Lewis, Human Resources Director
TO: All Employees
RE: Holiday Party
DATE: December 3

Regarding the note I received from a member of Alcoholics Anonymous requesting a non-drinking table, you didn't sign your name. I'm happy to accommodate this request, but if I put a sign on a table that reads, "AA"; you wouldn't be anonymous anymore. How am I supposed to handle this? Somebody? Forget about the gifts exchange, no gifts exchange are allowed since the union members feel that $10.00 is too much money and executives believe $10.00 is very little for a gift.

No gifts exchange will be allowed.

Patty

FROM: Patty Lewis, Human Resources Director
TO: All Employees
RE: Holiday Party
DATE: December 7

What a diverse group we are! I had no idea that December 20 begins the Muslim holy month of Ramadan, which forbids eating and drinking during daylight hours. There goes the party! Seriously, we can appreciate how a luncheon this time of year does not accommodate our Muslim employees' beliefs. Perhaps Luigi's can hold off on serving your meal until the end of the party—the days are so short this time of year—or else package everything for take home in little foil swans. Will that work?

Meanwhile, I've arranged for members of Overeaters Anonymous to sit farthest from the dessert buffet and pregnant women will get the table closest to the restrooms. Gays are allowed to sit with each other. Lesbians do not have to sit with Gay men, each will have their own table. Yes, there will be flower arrangement for the Gay men's table. To the person asking permission to cross dress, no cross dressing allowed though. We will have booster seats for short people. Low-fat food will be available for those on a diet. We cannot control the salt used in the food we suggest for those people with high blood pressure problems to taste first. There will be fresh fruits as dessert for Diabetics, the restaurant cannot supply
"no sugar" desserts. Sorry!
Did I miss anything?

Patty

FROM: Patty Lewis, Human Resources Director
TO: All Employees
RE: Holiday Party
DATE: December 8

So December 22 marks the Winter Solstice. What do you expect me to do, a tap-dance on your heads? Fire regulations at Luigi's prohibit the burning of sage by our "earth-based Goddess-worshipping" employees, but we'll try to accommodate your shamanic drumming circle during the band's breaks. Okay???

FROM: Patty Lewis, Human Resources Director
TO: All Employees
RE: Holiday Party
DATE: December 9

People, people, nothing sinister was intended by having our CEO dress up like Santa Claus! Even if the anagram of "Santa" does happen to be "Satan" there is no evil connotation to our own "little man in a red suit." It's a tradition, folks, like sugar shock at Halloween or family feuds over the Thanksgiving turkey or broken hearts on Valentine's Day.
Could we lighten up? Please? Also the company has changed their mind in announcing the special announcement at the gathering. You will get a notification in the mail sent to your home.

Patty

Straight talking	Politically Correct translation
Addiction	Pharmacological compulsion
Airhead	Reality detached
Alive	Metabolically abled
Bad speller	Lexically challenged
Bald	Comb-free Folically impaired
Bisexual	Sexually nonselective
Blind	Visually challenged
Body odour	Corporeal fragrance
Boring	Charm-free zone Non-engaging conversationalist
Bomb (car)	Mechanically challenged
Broken home	Dysfunctional family
Bum or hobo	Homeless person
Caretaker or janitor	Site engineer
Clumsy	Uniquely coordinated
Cranky	Approval disinterested
Crook	Ethically challenged Morally unencumbered Behaviourially challenged
Dead	Terminally inconvenienced Living impaired Mortally terminated Metabolically interrupted
Deaf	Visually oriented
Dirty old man	Chronologically differentiated sexual Gerontologically gifted male
Dishonest	Truth unencumbered Ethically disoriented
Drug addict	Chemically engaged
Drunk	Spacially disoriented Chemically inconvenienced

Fail	Achieve a negative success
Fat	Hyper-efficient metabolical life form Adipose enhanced Gravitationally challenged Horizontally challenged
Finger pointer	Blame transferer
Foreign food	Ethnic cuisine
Garbage man	Sanitation engineer Waste removal engineer
Geek	Socially challenged
Girl	Pre-womyn
Gossip	Speedy transmission of near factual information
Handicapped	Differently abled
Having PMT	Cyclically adjusted
Homeless	Residentially flexible Domicile nonspecific
Hooker	Sexual care provider
Housewife	Domestic care provider Domestic engineer
Ignorant	Factually unencumbered
Illegal aliens	Undocumented immigrants
Jailer	Custodial consultants
Jungle	Rainforest
Late	Rescheduled arrival time
Lazy	Motivationally unencumbered
Lumberjack	Tree reaper
Natural disaster	Global warming occurrence
Sex change	Gender re-assignment
Short	Vertically challenged
Shy	Conversationally selective
Spendthrift	Negative saver
Talkative	Verbally endowed

Tall	Vertically enhanced
Caravan park	Mobile home community
Ugly	Appearance diverse
Unemployed	Involuntarily leisured
Vagrant	Domiciliarly unattached
Worst	Least best
Wrong	Differently logical

Politically correct end of year greeting

Please accept with no obligation,
implied or implicit our best wishes for an
environmentally conscious,
socially responsible, low stress, non-addictive,
gender neutral, celebration of the winter solstice holiday,
practised within the most enjoyable traditions of the religious
persuasion of your choice,
or secular practices of your choice,
with respect for the religious/secular
persuasions and/or traditions of others,
or their choice not to practice
religious or secular traditions at all.
And a fiscally successful,
personally fulfilling, and medically
uncomplicated recognition of the onset
of the generally accepted calendar
year XXXX,
but not without due respect for the calendars
of choice of other
cultures whose contributions to society
have helped make England great, (not
to imply that England is necessarily greater
than any other country or is
the only "England" in the western hemisphere),
and without regard to the
race, creed, colour, age, physical ability, religious faith, choice of
computer platform, or sexual preference of the wishee.

PC glossary for describing women

She is not a **bleached blonde,** She is **peroxide dependent.**

She is not a **tart**, she is **imaginatively attired.**

She is not **mutton dressed up as lamb,** she is **age defiant.**

She is not suffering from **PMS,** she is **hormonally influenced.**

She is not a **bad cook**, She is **microwave compatible.**

She is not **half naked**, She is **frugal with her attire.**

She does not wear **too much jewellery,** She is **metallically overburdened.**

She is not **conceited**, she is **intimately aware of her best qualities**.

She does not **gain weight**, she is a **metabolic underachiever**.

She doesn't **shop till she drops**, she is **retail incessant**.

She is not a **screamer** or **moaner**, she is **vocally appreciative**.

She is not **self-centred**, she is **ego abundant**.

She is not **easy**, she is **horizontally accessible**.

She does not **tease** or **flirt**, she engages in **goal-detached provocation.**

She is not **too skinny**, she is **skeletally prominent**.

She does not **wear too much perfume**, she commits **fragrance abuse.**

She is not **kinky**, she is a **non-inhibited sexual companion**.

She does not wear **too much makeup**, she has reached **cosmetic saturation**.

She does not have **breast implants**, she is **gravity resistant**.

She doesn't have **big tits**, she is **mammarily endowed**.

She is not a **nag**, she is a **conscientious appellant**.

She is not a **shrew**, she is **overtly insistent**.

She doesn't **run at the mouth**, she is **linguistically gifted**.

She isn't **hairy legged**, she is **follicly endowed**.

She doesn't have a **big nose**, she has a **prominent proboscus**.

She is not **overly ambitious**, she is **excellence oriented**.

She is not a **gold digger**, she is **fiscally fond**.

She does not **overdo the makeup**, she **applies enhancement camouflage**.

She is not having a **bad hair day**, she is **temporarily mood altered**.

She does not suffer from the **green-eyed monster**, she has a **keen sense of possession**.

She is not a **brunette**, she is **blonde insufficient**.
She is not **overly critical**, she is a **paragon of discernment**.

PC glossary for describing men

He does not have a **beer gut**, he has developed a **liquid grain storage facility**.

He is not a **bad dancer**, he is **indiscrimately foot preferenced**.

He doesn't **get lost all the time**, he investigates **alternative destinations**.

He is not **balding**, he is in **follicle regression**.

He is not **hairy as a bath mat**, he is **follicle abundant**.

He is not **useless around the house**, he is **domestically oblivious**.

He is not a **cradle robber**, he prefers **generationally differential relationships**.

He does not get **falling-down drunk**, he becomes **accidentally horizontal**.

He does not act like a **total ass**, he develops a case of **rectal-cranial inversion**.

He is not a **sex machine**, he is **romantically automated**.

He is not a **male chauvinist pig**, he has **swine empathy**.

He does not **undress you with his eyes**, he has an **introspective pornographic moment**.

He is not afraid of **commitment**, he is **monogamously challenged**.

He is not **insensitive**, he is **prompt incoherent**.

He is not a **couch potato**. He is a **sedentary root vegetable**.

He is not a **hog** with the **remote control**, he is a **prominently proficient RC user**.

He is not having a **midlife crisis**, he is **assessing his chronological options**.

He is not a **dirty old man**, he is a **gender enthusiastic geriatric**.

He is not **emotionally insensitive**, he is **blissfully unaware**.

He doesn't **forget anniversaries**, he **omits remembering specific occasions**.

He is not a **workaholic**, he is a **career enthusiast**.

He is not an **alcoholic**, he is **beverage attuned**.

He is not **taciturn**, he is **linguistically sparing**.

He is not **domineering**, he is an **alpha-placed humanoid**.

He isn't **quick tempered**, he is **emotionally free range**.

He isn't a **skirt chaser**, he is **acutely other-gender attuned**.

He isn't **slow off the mark**, he is **cerebrally challenged**.

He isn't **getting grumpy**, he's **expressing non-core feelings.**

Politically correct cat definitions

My cat does not barf hairballs; he is a floor/rug redecorator.

My cat does not break things; she helps gravity do its job.

My cat does not fear dogs; they are merely sprint practice tools.

My cat does not gobble; she eats with alacrity.

My cat does not scratch; he is a furniture/rug/skin ventilator.

My cat does not yowl; he is singing off-key.

My cat is not a "shedding machine"; she is a hair relocation stylist.

My cat is not a "treat-seeking missile"; she enjoys the proximity of food.

My cat is not a bed hog; he is a mattress appreciator.

My cat is not a chatterbox; she is advising me on what to do next.

My cat is not a dope addict; she is catnip appreciative.

My cat is not a lap fungus; he is bed selective.

My cat is not a pest; she is attention deprived.

My cat is not a ruthless hunter; she is a wildlife control expert.

My cat is not evil; she is badness enhanced.

My cat is not fat; he is mass enhanced.

My cat is not hydrophobic; she has an inability to appreciate moisture.

My cat is not lazy; he is motivationally challenged.

My cat is not underfoot; she is shepherding me to my next destination, the food dish.

A History of Math Lessons

Math Lessons 1950 to date.

Teaching Maths in 1950:
A logger sells a truckload of lumber for $100. His cost of production is 4/5 of the price. What is his profit?

Teaching Maths in 1960:
A logger sells a truckload of lumber for $100. His cost of production is 4/5 of the price, or $80. What is his profit?

Teaching Maths in 1970:
A logger exchanges a set "L" of lumber for a set "M" of money. The cardinality of set "M" is 100. Each element is worth one dollar. The set "C", the cost of production contains 20 fewer points than set "M". What is the cardinality of the set "P" of profits?

Teaching Maths in 1980:
A logger sells a truckload of lumber for $100. His cost of production is $80 and his profit is $20.
Your assignment: Underline the number 20.

Teaching Maths in 1990:
By cutting down beautiful forest trees, the logger makes $20. What do you think of this way of making a living? Topic for class participation: How did the forest birds and squirrels feel as the logger cut down the trees? There are no wrong answers.

Teaching Maths in 1993:
By laying off 402 of its loggers, a company improves its stock price from $80 to $100. How much capital gain per share does the CEO make by exercising his stock options at $80? Assume capital gains are no longer taxed, because this encourages investment.

Teaching Maths in 1997:
A company outsources all of its loggers. They save on benefits and when demand for their product is down the logging work force can easily be cut back. The average logger employed by the company earned $50,000, had 3 weeks vacation, received a nice retirement plan and medical insurance. The contracted logger charges $50 an hour. Was outsourcing a good move?

Teaching Maths in the new millennium:
A logging company exports its wood-finishing jobs to its Indonesian subsidiary and lays off the corresponding half of its US workers (the higher-paid half). It clear-cuts 95% of the forest, leaving the rest for the spotted owl, and lays off all its remaining US workers. It tells the workers that the spotted owl is responsible for the absence of fellable trees and lobbies Congress for exemption from the Endangered Species Act. Congress instead exempts the company from all federal regulation. What is the return on investment of the lobbying?

Pees and Queues, Eyes and Tees

Michelle O'Regan

Please save us

From the barren and morbid landscape of
Political correctness,
The proctal fastidiousness of minding our Qs and Ps
The mincing pedantry of dotting our Is and crossing our Ts.

Moral righteousness
Fiscal rectitude
Weapons of mass deception
Machine model efficiencies
Papal infallibility
Models of excellence.

Party poopers
All!!

Squeezing the last juices out of living
Turning us all into automatons
And mindless zombies.

While common sense,
Old wives tales
And decency
Huddle under a rickety bridge—
hags and winos,
Disdained and vilified.

And
Devil-may-careness
Riggishness
Irreverence
And
Joyful exuberance
Have all been banished
To an island gulag.

Managers, Their Mission and Mumbo Jumbo

"So much of what we call management
consists in making it difficult for people to work"

Peter F Drucker

The realities of the contemporary workplace, continuous improvement, downsizing, re-engineering, casualisation, off shoring, have been the corporate processes used to divest workers of job satisfaction and job security. Finding oneself dehired, cashiered or surplused—all euphemisms for being sacked—is a distinct possibility in this working environment.

Sinister euphemisms are part of the management mumbo jumbo to persuade the staff that "wrong is right", "black is white" and "false is true". They sack hundreds of workers and call it "trimming the corporate fat" and "removing the deadwood". But CEO and executive salary packages are increased incrementally and it's called "adding value for the shareholder".

In many cases, the company or organisation's Mission and Vision Statements and much of the management jargon is inane and meaningless. This whole area of bureaucratic zerospeak has made sawdust out of terms such as "enhance", "initiate", "facilitate" "integrate" and "empower".

"There's no 'I' in 'team'.
But then there's no 'I' in 'useless smug colleague' either.
And there are four in 'platitude-quoting idiot'."

Terms such as "doing more with less", "working smarter not harder" and all the use of Positive Thinking strategies for indoctrinating staff to go the extra mile in their work are being invoked because in effect when workforces are downsized, rightsized, brightsized this amounts to fewer 'bums on seats' having to continue to conduct the business of that company with less resources. The propaganda sold to the worker serves much the same purpose as the whip cracking over the slave's back in the cotton fields or in the bowels of the galley.

One slight glimmer of optimism for the future is that language, reflecting the ebullience of human spirit, can bounce back. The pervasiveness of the Net has meant that newly coined terms find that crevice, that foothold, like daisies springing out of the cracks in miles of concreted carpark. In the final section of the book, Truspeak, you will find 'Korporatese' which may go some way to renewing your faith in the resilience and exuberance of language.

Mission Statements

"Words are the tools of thought, and you will often find that you are thinking badly because you are using the wrong tools, trying to bore a hole with a screw-driver, or draw a cork with a coal-hammer".

What a Word!, 1935
A P Herbert

"It is our mission to assertively supply unique solutions while continuing enthusiastically to administrate world-class materials and quickly leverage others' value-added benefits so that we may endeavour to competently integrate scalable paradigms for 100 per cent customer satisfaction."

Can you guess by the language what exemplary organization this could be? A bank, a penitentiary, a hospital? Sorry to disappoint – it's Domino's Pizza, the ones with the dots on the box and what amounts to a loss of the plot.

Mission statements were intended to shine like a beacon for the managers and staff into the future, illuminating the road ahead so that they could clearly direct all their energies to effect their vision. However when the motherhood statement is written in such generic mumbo jumbo, even the jumbos would have a problem lumbering through the jungle on any mission.

Examples are:

We have committed to efficiently simplify seven-habits-conforming products and competently disseminate quality information to set us apart from the competition.

Our goal is to efficiently revolutionize quality opportunities in order to collaboratively administrate performance based leadership skills.

Our mission is to continue to efficiently provide access to timely sources.

Our mission is to completely customize cutting edge technology and efficiently foster corporate resources to meet our customer's needs network high-quality content to meet our customer's needs.

Our mission is to interactively provide access to high-quality catalysts for change so that we may authoritatively utilize timely deliverables for 100% customer satisfaction.

We have committed to authoritatively restore cutting edge infrastructures.

We have committed to enthusiastically build unique meta-services to set us apart from the competition.

Our mission is to continue to pro actively fashion seven-habits-conforming materials to meet our customer's needs.

It is our job to seamlessly promote low-risk high-yield infrastructures in order that we may collaboratively enhance effective leadership skills while promoting personal employee growth.

Choose from these Corporate Fuzzy words

If you want to manufacture your own wonderful sounding mission statements and impress management no end with your grasp of the buzzwords, choose from the following:

Adverbs
quickly, pro actively, efficiently, assertively, interactively, professionally, authoritatively, conveniently, completely, continually, dramatically, enthusiastically, collaboratively, synergistically, seamlessly, competently, globally.

Verbs
maintain, supply, provide access to, disseminate, network, create, engineer, integrate, leverage other's, leverage existing, coordinate, administrate, initiate, facilitate, promote, restore, fashion, revolutionize, build, enhance, simplify, pursue, utilize, foster, customize, negotiate.

Adjectives
professional, timely, effective, unique, cost effective, virtual, scalable, economically sound, inexpensive, value-added, business, quality, diverse, high-quality, competitive, excellent, innovative, corporate, high standards in, world-class, error-free, performance based, multimedia based, market-driven, cutting edge, high-payoff, low-risk high-yield, long-term high-impact, prospective, progressive, ethical, enterprise-wide, principle-centered, mission-critical, parallel, interdependent, emerging, seven-habits-conforming, resource-leveling.

Nouns
content, paradigms, data, opportunities, information, services, materials, technology, benefits, solutions, infrastructures, products, deliverables, catalysts for change, resources, methods of empowerment, sources, leadership skills, meta-services, intellectual capital.

"Working with the passion, commitment, enthusiasm, committed to teamwork to fulfil our company needs"

Mission statement of a sticky note manufacturer

Now compare it to -

"We use our time to enhance our skills with the passion and desire of self-fulfillment."

The CIA's mission statement.

- A mission statement by web design firm Anadrom Ltd (www.anadrom.net)

'Please browse the site to see our full range of services, we can remain customer focused and goal-directed, innovate and be an inside-out organization which facilitates sticky web-readiness transforming turnkey eyeballs to brand 24/365 paradigms with benchmark turnkey channels implementing viral e-services and dot-com action-items while we take that action item off-line and raise a red flag and remember touch base as you think about the red tape outside of the box and seize B2B e-tailers and re-envisioneer innovative partnerships that evolve dot-com initiatives delivering synergistic earballs to incentivise.'

Ethical Canary

Wouldn't it be great?
Wouldn't it be fine?

To have a job specification
In any corporation
For
"An ethical canary"?

Said "canary"
Paid to attend
Meetings,
Brainstorms,
Policy pontifications
Procedural deliberations…
Function being
To turn yellow, flutter one's proverbial wings
And with a resounding
THUNK!!
Land one's head upon
Boardroom table.
Whenever matters
Take a course
That will mean the
Workplace has suddenly become
Dangerously toxic
To all who
Work on the coalface
Of said industry.

Think of the lives
That might be saved!

Peter Principle:

In every hierarchy, whether it be government or business, each employee tends to rise to his level of incompetence; every post tends to be filled by an employee incompetent to execute its duties.

Corollaries:

1. Incompetence knows no barriers of time or place.
2. Work is accomplished by those employees who have not yet reached their level of incompetence.
3. If at first you don't succeed, try something else.

How many chiefs? Now that the Indians have been downsized

Never before in our history have we been so few led by so many, systems have been 'operationally improved' and have generated these job titles:

- Chief Nuclear Officer
- Chief Procurement Officer
- Chief Information Officer
- Chief Learning Officer
- Chief Transformation Officer
- Chief Cultural Officer
- Chief People Officer
- Chief Ethics Officer
- Chief Turnaround Officer
- Chief Technology Officer
- Chief Creative Officer

One wonders if they have also recruited a "Chief Officer for inventing Chief Officer Titles!" Is the way the American Indian created the names for their chiefs—Chief Running Bear, Chief Sitting Bull, Chief Hunting Wolf and so on...

But there are other job titles that are becoming 'diversified', is this a way of fooling the worker into believing that their job is substantively different from what it was?

Examples are:

Travel agent: travel counsellor, vacation specialist, destination counsellor, reservation specialist

Salesman: relationship manager

Bill collector: persistency specialist

There are further examples of how euphemism and doublespeak are used. For instance 'worst driver' or 'worst employee' are removed and replaced with 'least best'. Bribes and graft are called 'rebates' and 'fees for product testing'.

And this one which is a classic—a bank in Texas transformed a robbery of an ATM machine into an 'unauthorised transaction'.

Automotive graveyards can be termed 'auto dismantlers and recyclers' and toxic waste dumps can be retitled 'Ecology Inc'.

Management speak and what it really means

Manager Says	What it really means
I advise you	I'm ordering you
I don't totally disagree with you	Even if you are right, I don't care
We have an opportunity	You have a problem
This will prove challenging	A dirty job nobody wants
In a perfect world	Just get it done and no complaints!
Help me to understand	You're not making sense and I'm not listening anyway
You need to see the 'big picture'	Nod vigorously, this is an edict from Above.
Whereas I appreciate your contribution	But it's not going to carry any weight
The committee couldn't reach consensus	It was so heated it nearly came to blows.

Here's an exciting opportunity	Be afraid, be very afraid!
My door is always open	That doesn't mean I have any time to listen to your lame ideas.
We have to put on our marketing hats	Leave the ethics at the door
I'm glad you asked me that	The PR department have scripted an answer
Human resources	Like the world's resources, a commodity of no account, to be used and abused
The upcoming downsizing will benefit most employees	They will benefit me and I'm the only one that counts
Value-added	Very expensive
We need to form a sub-committee	Because it isn't in our interests to resolve it now
I'll never lie to you	The truth is a flexible commodity
Continuous improvement is our goal	Just when you learned how to do your job, you'll have to learn to do it differently
We aim to be an employer of choice	Things won't change but the PR will improve
Performance reviews are good management practice	It gives us an excuse to make you squirm
I'd like your input on this	I'm looking for a scapegoat when this goes pear-shaped
We have to leverage our resources	You're working overtime, unpaid of course
We need to stay competitive	Means pay cuts and loss of conditions for employees
We have a new paradigm	We're changing all titles for jobs and departments. Why? Because that's what managers do

We plan to institute a rewards and recognition program	The brown-nosers and "Yes" men will receive high praise, even advancement
We believe in consulting with staff	We tell you what we're going to do, then we do it!
I want you to go the extra mile on this project	Forget the family and the footy and friends, you are homing from work on this one!
Our vision and mission...	The kind of stuff we can write on stationery and business cards
There's been a paradigm shift	We missed the latest management fad and now we're playing catch up
We will follow the agenda, any items you wish to discuss can be raised in "Other business"	By that time you will be hypnotised, lobotomised and anaesthetised and will be dying to cut the meeting short
Let's hit the ground running	Don't bother thinking too much first
We plan to empower staff	We'll find some cappos who will be in charge of restructuring and selling out their colleagues
Our objectives are concrete and transparent	Ah, the paradox of management speak! It beats quantum physics
At the end of the day	Sentence starter with the meaning of a fart
Our key performance indicators	Statistics kept to measure what exactly?
Let's agree to move on	I don't feel comfortable talking about this fiasco.

Now we need to regroup	Managers retain their jobs whilst lowly heads roll
We like team players in this organisation	Herd mentality over critical thinking any day.
What's our fallback position?	Did we have a Plan B? Well did we?
Hard work and contribution does not go unnoticed	Your efforts won't go unpunished – you look as though you want my job!
I won't go into 'solution mode'	I haven't got a bloody clue just yet
You need to work smarter not harder	Don't tell me about huge workloads – complain and you could be up for poor performance
You are frontline customer service staff	You do 90% of the work and take 100% of the blame when someone complains
We have a strong customer focus	We say we do to impress customers but all we care about is profit
Our employees are our greatest asset	Believe that and you'll believe anything
We believe in transparency and accountability	...and Santa Claus and the Tooth fairy
Keep negative comments to a minimum	I don't want to hear any disagreement on this
We have made a commitment to this	Only for as long as it takes to put it to bed, and as long as it doesn't take up too many of our resources.

Employment contract

A proposed employment contract for management consultants Gleeds Group

13. Waiver

'No forbearance of failure by the Employer at any time to require performance of any provision of the Agreement or to enforce strictly the obligations of the Employee or to take action to suspend the Employee or to determine the Agreement forthwith upon discovering cause therefore shall effect the right of the Employer so to do any time and no waiver by the Employer of any condition or breach of any clause whether by conduct or otherwise shall constitute a continuing or further waiver of any such condition or breach or as the breach of any other clause.'

Job ads decoded

Competitive Salary:
We are a lean organization, meaning all excess fat has been trimmed from wages.

Join our fast-paced company:
Don't expect an induction or training. Hit the ground running and stay running.

Casual work atmosphere:
We don't pay you enough to dress up, but that doesn't mean you mustn't.

Deadline-oriented:
From day one you'll be behind and you'll never catch up.

Some overtime required:
A few hours each night and some also on weekends.

Duties will vary:
You will be taking instructions from anyone and everyone in the office.

Must have an eye for detail:
We don't check it so you have to... why? Because you'll be blamed if anything is missed.

Career-minded:
Women applicants must be childless and remain that way.

Apply in person:
If you're ugly, fat, old or a bad dresser, we'll tell you the position has already been filled.

No phone calls please:
We've already filled the position but we have to be seen to be advertising externally. Send us your résumé and we'll throw it in the bin.

Seeking candidates with a wide variety of experience:
You will be needed to fill the position of three people who've just been fired.

Problem-solving skills a must:
The company you're applying to is in a perpetual state of mayhem.

Good Communication skills:
Managers make motherhood statements and you must read between the lines.

A real job Advertisement

Example, a real job ad in Weekend Australian August 20-21 2005

Sector and Thematic Specialists

Duties
- Review and evaluate projects
- Cultivate cooperation
- Serve as a focal point
- Forge links and networks
- Advocate, facilitate, educate
- Develop knowledge products
- Develop expertise
- Develop policy
- Formulate and process loans and technical assistance projects
- Advise and assist
- Contribute to achieving the Millennium Development Goals

Demonstrated Abilities

- Strong interdisciplinary competence and significant experience in one or more of the fields listed and familiarity with cross-cutting operational issues such as poverty reductions, human development, good governance and environmental concerns.
- Loan processing and project implementation.
- Knowledge in formulating strategies and preparing feasibility studies.
- For transport and energy roles, competence in engineering designs and cost estimates, procurement and administration of civil engineering projects.

What is this job? Does the person going for the position require a degree in mumbo jumbo to understand what it's about?
A tiny logo in the corner gives an indication, "Asian Development Bank" Maybe it's a teller's position!

Corporate Irony

The company I worked for had an employee-suggestion competition, the entire staff was to submit entries that would save money for the firm.

The winner was a man in my department who suggested we post corporate memos on bulletin boards, instead of printing 200 individual copies for distribution. He got a helium balloon with the company logo and one share of stock.

A memo announcing the prize went out to 200 people.

A 'Real' Job Application

Name:
Tanya Hoolihan

Sex:
Not yet. Still waiting for the right person.

Desired Position:
Look I'll take anything that pays me more than I'm worth. But ideally, I'd like to be in a position where I didn't have to work at all.

Desired Salary:
Let's haggle. I'd obviously like a great deal more than you'll offer.

Education:
Basic but yes.

Last position held:
Scapegoat for upper management.

Most Notable Achievement:
Being able to go from job to job without learning too much about words or numbers.

Reason for leaving:
I got bored.

Hours available to work:
Not picky.

Preferred Hours:
1:30-3:30 p.m., Monday, Tuesday, and Thursday.

Do you have any special skills?
Yes but I don't think that's any of your business.

May we contact your current employer?
You could if I had one.

Do you have any physical conditions that would prohibit you from working in an office environment?
It depends on what they do in offices.

Do you have a car?
Maybe you should ask me if the car I have goes.

Have you received any special awards or recognition?
I buy a X Lotto ticket every week and one time down the pub I won $30 on Keno.

Do you smoke?
Only when I get a chance.

What would you like to be doing in five years?
I'd like to be living off a sugar daddy by then so I won't have to work any more. But if the opportunity comes up before five years is up, then you'll understand if I hand in my notice.

Do you certify that the above is true and complete to the best of your knowledge?
To the best of my ability I have been totally truthful.

Sign Here:
Scorpio

If Résumés Told the Truth

Objective
To find a way to get paid every week whilst staring at a computer screen and looking busy when the supervisor passes.

Education
Sketchy—went to posh school but wasn't exactly a shining light. Taught that it's not what you know, but who you know.

Employment
Network Management (10/2004—Present)
Became highly skilled in selecting TV programs so that I could avoid ads, informercials and chose to watch a continuous feed of Law and Order and Forensic series.

Debt Consolidation (5/2002—9/2004)
Managed after getting myself in debt over mobile phone and credit card, to find a way to roll it all into one invoice which could safely be sent monthly to my father.

Resident distributor (3/2000—4/2002)
Made a living from dealing in recreational drugs.

Computer Skills
On/off switch * Computer games * Surfing the net.

Honours and Awards
*Runner up in prettiest baby contest.
*Won tickets to go see Kylie on a radio call up quiz.
*Got the winning door prize at the pub—a basket of goodies.

If you want references, it's best to ask my mum or my boyfriend. They both know what to say.

Answering the tough interview questions
(suck-up responses that get your foot in the door)

Remember, shiny shoes, a firm handshake and eye contact, mirror the body language of the one on the panel asking you the question. Act as if you already work with them and this is merely incidental, a test of your mental acuity at avoiding the land mines that sadistic interviewers like posing for unsuspecting mortals.

If there were a situation at work, how would you handle the conflict?

You have to appear to be a realist, even though you are about to enter a Theme Park they call the Workplace so "I know everything cannot run smoothly at work all the time. When there is a conflict I usually try to determine the source of the problem and see if it can be solved. This might involve other members of the work team discussing the problem and offering possible solutions. I would then try to pick the solution which appears to have the best outcome and put it into action."

Tell us a story.

Obviously he doesn't mean the Three Bears unless you were going for a job as the Bear's Housekeeper- no this is a thinking on your feet exercise to test if you're going to fit in to their work culture—so make it a Politically Correct Story of the Three Bears if you have to, or some demonstration that you keep the positive principle going, that despite adversity you still keep smiling, that you are a team player etcetera, etcetera. Make the story about yourself not Livingstone or Mawson and their feats of exploration.

If you were a merry-go-round what song would you be playing? And if you were an animal on the merry-go-round what animal would you be?

This is a question about teamwork, your capacity for creativity (which will soon be put to sleep but works at interview) and the

kind of animal you choose will tell them psychometrically what kind of 'animal' you are.
Choosing a giraffe will indicate you have the 'big picture' in mind—your song could be "On a Clear Day You Can See Forever"; choosing a wolf might be a nice touch especially if you explain that they are such good team players and your song could be "All for One and One for All!" Don't be a lemming or a wildebeest or even a zebra, yes they do move in large groups but they are inclined to be eaten by other animals further up the food chain and rush over cliffs, and you don't want to give them any notion that you are that much of a suck up or a team player!

What does "customer service" mean to you?

Bite down on any choice anecdotes about being on the receiving end of "customer service" You have to think fast, think on your feet again, have an anecdote ready of an example or two of customer service. It would be no harm if you were the one delivering it, and how you went the extra mile for that total stranger.

The customer coming to the counter at two minutes before closing time, how it was an incredibly complex request however you could see how important a matter it was to the customer. So you attended with the best of grace and of course a smile and warmth worthy of dealing with your favourite relative, and having gone the extra mile, the customer was effusive in their gratitude, blah, blah, blah.

What are some of the things you find difficult to do?

They don't want to hear that you find everything is plain sailing. Once again they want to hear how you have overcome fear say for public speaking, or confronting someone difficult and how you handled yourself. They want to know how you overcome adversity or personal blocks to your putting your goals and dreams into realities. Pick a little parable about having your back up against the wall, fear in your belly, everyone relying on you and how you saved the day, the human equivalent to the "Little Red Engine that Could".

Tell me about a time when you tried and failed?

Don't for heaven's sake tell them you never did, because even if that were true, they don't want to hear it. They want a bleeding heart story. So tell them how you trained and trained to win the running race at school, (don't mention anything academic, you don't want them thinking you are deficient in that area). And how you lost the race, but then later you got an award for being the best improver, and how that effected all the other things you tried in life. This will achieve the effect you want.

What are your short and long term goals?

Don't make the mistake of assuming they think you have another life outside of work, or that you could conceivably be only here for the pay packet (heaven forbid!). The answer has to be as if you plan to eat, drink and breathe this organisation for the foreseeable future. Short term to learn everything you can about the job to make you effective and just as important to get to network with as many staff as possible. Long term you must impress them that you are a go-getter but don't overdo it, they don't want to feel their own jobs are threatened. Being the best you can be, of service to others etc that kind of theme will work nicely.

If your friends were standing round your grave, how would they describe you?

Ah, good question! "Well I think they'd be sorry I was gone, because I was always the non-drinking mate who'd take them out and drive them home safely. Also I would make them a loan when they were short before payday—so yes they'd be missing me."

If you had to live your life all over again, what would you change?

Watch out for this one, it's a minefield. Like a corporation, don't admit mistakes if you can possibly avoid it. "Well I don't believe in regrets. We have to live in the present and face forward into the future. Life is a continuous learning process and I'm learning all the time, so I wouldn't be inclined to change anything. I'm very happy with where I am right now, sitting in this room with you, having an opportunity to persuade you that I am the best candidate for this job."

"There are two kinds of people in life:
people who like their jobs,
and people who don't work here anymore."

Dear Hiring Manager,

Thank you for your letter of March 16. After careful consideration, I regret to inform you that I am unable to accept your refusal to offer me a position in your department at this time. This year I have been particularly fortunate in receiving an unusually large number of rejection letters. With such a varied and promising field of candidates, it is impossible for me to accept all refusals.

Despite your company's outstanding qualifications and previous experience in rejecting applicants, I find that your rejection does not meet my needs at this time. Therefore, I will assume the position in your department this August. I look forward to seeing you then. Best of luck in rejecting future applicants.

Management styles

1) Managing by keeping in front of the posse
"We'll have to talk" you can hear them say, just as they have disappeared around the corner.

2) Managing by window gazing
When you talk to them, their thoughts keep staring out of the windows. It's a tip they must have picked up from daytime soaps.

3) Managing by Post-its'
These managers want to impress you with their active listening skills by continuously writing on Post-it's while you are talking.

4) Managing by delegation to factotum
The secretary or PA becomes the doer and decider. This is a cunning ploy. If things go well, the manager looks good, if not he has someone to blame.

5) Managing by knowing nothing
"I want your thoughts on the matter." They let YOU give answers. And they waffle away with anecdotes that are not on task.

6) Managing by Conceptual Thinking
Big picture why this won't work managers. The idea that this never will work, completely satisfies them: They will always have something to talk about.

7) Managing by hiding information
Information is power. Be very thankful to get any information at all. This person operates like the CIA on a needs-to-know basis.

8) Managing by doing exactly what the boss says
These managers don't encourage their bosses to 'think outside the square', they know this would lead to more work. They are firm adherers to the status quo.

9) Managing by walking one foot behind the boss
Understanding the pecking order and etiquette of the spoken or unspoken organization will go far. Two steps behind your immediate superior will make him/her think more kindly of you.

10) Managing by smiling and wearing nice suits
Learning to shout drinks in happy hour, to wear good clothes and conversational ties is a big help in advancing his career.

11) Managing by studying

This lot spend all their time in courses and attending seminars—not so they can become better managers—only to avoid the hands-on stuff.

12) Managing by creating vague overhead sheets

The flow chart, Powerpoint gurus who dazzle with what appears to be savvy.

13) Managing by open door and empty room

Oh yes there's an open door policy but there's no one at home ever. He's a corridor warrior with his name down for all the sub committees and work groups.

14) Managing by speaking with other managers

Here's one that is very popular. By conferring with other managers much time is expended and something that could have been accomplished in fifteen minutes by talking to a lower echelon employee.

15) Managing by having a non-supporting infrastructure

These managers have their 'raison d'être' the non-supportive infrastructure so it's in their interest not to improve on the system that justifies their existence.

16) BUA management (by using abbreviations)

This management style is ATRASACWOC (Adopted To Reach A Shorter And Clearer Way Of Communication).

17) Managing by using buzz words

The sultans of spin and the bwanas of buzz, these managers ensure that they enhance everything they leverage with buzzwords to dazzle.

18) Managing by reorganization

Never let it be said that you are too organized. If it's organized, then reorganize.

19) Managing by believing
These managers have a strong belief that it will all turn out well. Not based on any pragmatic evidence but a strong abiding belief none the less.

20) Managing by forgetting promises
They promise you they will attend to this or that and as they do they look you straight in the eye. When you ask in a couple of weeks about progress they say they've been busy, remind them again what it was about. Not a good sign.

Tom Swifties of the Workplace

You could only find jokes more cheesy than these if you worked at a cheese factory...

Q. How's your job at the clock company?
A. Only time will tell.

Q. How's your job at the banana company?
A. I keep slipping up.

Q. How's your job on the new highway?
A. I'm so busy I don't know which way to turn.

Q. How's your job at the travel agency?
A. I'm going nowhere.

Q. How's your job at the swivel chair company?
A. It makes my head spin!

Q. How's your job at the lemon juice company?
A. I've had bitter jobs.

Q. How's your job at the pie company?
A. It didn't pan out.

Q. How's your job at the balloon factory?
A. We can't keep up with inflation.

Q. How's your job at the crystal ball company?
A. I'm making a fortune.

Q. How's your job at the history book company?
A. There's no future in it.

Q. How's your job at the clock company?
A. I'm having second thoughts about it.

Q. How's your job on the farm?
A. Problems keep cropping up.

Q. How's your job at the sewing shop?
A. Hanging on by a thread.

Q. How's your job at the eye glasses clinic?
A. I have clear job objectives.

Yuletide CEO announces reforms

Newly appointed CEO of the struggling Yuletide Corporation, Ake Hahnberger, has announced that the North Pole Division will be rationalised.

Outsourcing of labour will mean a significant number of Elves will lose work, and it is likely horses will be phased in to replace the more expensive reindeer.

"It is a harsh measure," he said at a press conference in Helsinki yesterday, "but one that is very necessary."

The controversial measure of making Santa Claus a user-pays system is also being proposed. Mr Hahnberger said that the "welfarism of gift giving is a hopelessly redundant system based on the outmoded socialist model that died with the USSR in 1989."

He also announced plans to make Santa Claus redundant and replace him with cheaper overseas labour. Manufacturing and distribution of gifts would now be conducted from Mexico with some novelty pencil manufacturing being moved to China.

Santa Claus could not be contacted for comment, but rumour has it that he is in contract negotiations with Microsoft Corporation to star in a new advertising campaign for Windows 2000. Rudolph the Red-nosed Reindeer's future with Yuletide Corp is also uncertain.

Beating meeting blues

Do you find it hard to stay awake and alert at meetings and seminars? What about the long-winded conference calls when you are only attending to every dozenth word and as a result it's not making much sense? Are you sick and tired of hearing monotonous, meaningless deliberations which make you desperate to want to end it all with the nearest pointy pencil? Well here's the antidote to all that.

1. Be prepared. Make up enough supplies to get you through the month. Draw up a piece of card with 5 X 5 squares and write in these following suggested Bingo terms.

2. Print out or duplicate the following grid:

Exciting	Engaged	Core competencies	Paradigm	Triple bottom line
Enhance	Synchronise diaries	Corporate culture	24 / 7	Best-of breed-
Value-added	80-20 rule	Think outside the box	Can-do	Challenging
Result-driven	Empower	Knowledge base	Infrastructure	Mission & vision
Outcomes	Client focus	Holistic view	Game plan	Leverage

3. As you hear the terms being used, check them off.

4. If you manage to get five terms vertically, horizontally or diagonally shout with great gusto "Bullshit!!"

Corporate Clichés – A Cynic's Commentary

Mission statement

Supposedly a motherhood statement by the company or organization stating its values, objectives and strategies. However, the use of such vague weasel words as showing in 'Mission Statements' makes you wonder why the idea of taking this step has become so popular. At best it's window dressing, at its worst it is gobbledygook and even the employees aren't fooled.

Synergy

Based on the idea that the result is greater than the sum of its parts. The value in collaborative efforts producing quality solutions or at least that's what they'd have you believe.

Benchmarking

Supposedly when a company compares its business practices and so on with other competitors. However it isn't always "apples with apples" and oft time 'benchmarking' is utilised as a tool to leverage services and positions out of the organisation and outsource them because it was demonstrated that they were not competitive.

Customer-interfacing

The frontline of customer service, those on the coalface of human interaction with the customer.

Job satisfaction

Nearly an oxymoron these days, even though there is more and more of the doublespeak proclaiming that the workplace is exciting and engaging and challenging, the worker feels disempowered, disenfranchised and harassed much of the time. Also there is less and less tenure in occupations. The move towards casualisation is quite alarming in some countries, Spain being the fastest to casualise, Australia coming next. Not knowing whether you'll still be in your job next week does not help when you are speaking in terms of 'job satisfaction'.

80-20 rule

This was an economic theorem about wealth called Pareto's Law, how 80% of the world's wealth was in 20% of the world's pockets. But as these things are inclined to do all too often, its influence spread and it has been loosely quoted in many a boardroom when doing time and motion studies.

Best-of-breed

"We commodify best-of-breed infrastructure installations", our computer stuff is better than other peoples'. There's a problem with this, no one claims to come in second in this Dog Show. No consolation prizes at all, they are all best-of-breed!

Blended

"Our blended solutions achieve product excellence" means a mongrel of bits and pieces borrowed from other products.

Bottom line

In new managerese, this can mean more than the financial outcomes, it can mean 'reality'. "The bottom line is that we need to restructure and streamline our staffing arrangements" which more than likely means layoffs.

Can-do

"Can-do attitude is what we need in this company", in other words a good servant who does the hard yards without complaint.

Challenging

Oh what a lovely euphemism! It really means difficult sometimes nigh impossible. If it's used to describe a member of staff it most likely means they are frustratingly hard to handle from a manager's perspective.

Core competencies

This is what the organisation considers it does better than its competitors "We must leverage our core competencies" is managerese for 'we must do more of the things we're good at'.

24/7

Every blessed hour of the day every day of the week.

Holistic view

Appeals to our New Ageyness but what does it mean exactly?

Gifting

When you take home some corporate trash that's "gifting" it to you.

Move on

'I think the public wants to move on.' John Howard, PM, preferring not to discuss children overboard in the lead up to the 2004 election.

Feasibility

A lot of money is thrown at the you-beaut feasibility studies which supposedly establish whether a thing can work or not.

End/close of play

Can't you just say finish instead of using another sporting term?

Fight the tide

To argue your point against others, to swim when there's a rip.

Performance manage out

When unhappy with an employee you wrap it up in euphemistic terms, you don't even have to sack, dismiss or fire them. You make a case against the worker's efficiency and effectiveness.

Unpack

As in: "We need to unpack the issue" to take it out of its wrappings and trappings to do what I don't know, certainly not to gain any clarity or get closer to the truth.

Could not see the wood for the trees

Duh! Nonsense! As what are the trees made of?

Eggs in one basket

Old cliché about not putting all your faith in one strategy.

Cover it off

When someone more important agrees with you.

Caveat

A Latin term meaning 'condition'.

Cast the net

Speaking to the people, but only if all else fails.

Broaden our horizons

Extend out to the 'bigger picture'.

Hit the ground running

Act more, think less.

Damage Limitation

I've bolloxed this up and need to hide the truth.

Indicative

No one quite knows what this means but it's a good sounding word.

Fall down the cracks

Gets hopelessly lost. Employees' rights and conditions fall down the cracks when there's a restructure going on.

Capacity release

'Reduce staffing numbers'... sack 'em!

Incentive plans

The various strategies for motivating staff to work even harder. The "Employee of the month" scheme is used in the fast food industry and also retail outlets. Some managers would claim that getting paid for your work and staying in your job are incentive enough.

Chapter 7/Chapter 11

When a company's filing for bankruptcy there are two ways it can be done. Chapter 11, where the company is allowed to stay in operation while it attempts to pull back from the brink. Chapter 7, where the company has to close down and have its assets liquidated so that it can cover the debt.

Employee Stock Ownership Plan (ESOP)

A strategy for the employees of a company to invest in shares with that same company. This is an incentive plan used by some companies to motivate their employees. It was also used when companies were threatened with closure and the staff banded together and took out a syndicate.

Intellectual property

The inventor or creator has legal rights over their work or ideas but must be legally done through patents and copyrights. However, where that scientist or IT person works for a company there is often a clause in the employment contract that states the intellectual property belongs to the employer.

Strategic planning

Managers love to spend a significant part of their time planning for the future, where to go and how to get there. However with the language tools they have and the minds attracted to management positions, the mission and vision and corporate plans can often read like impossible-to-decipher mumbo-jumbo.

Outsource

When a service is taken out-of-house, usually follows quite logically that the organisation doesn't need as many staff, so more sackings.

Responsible

A very irresponsibly used term. If the managers and executives are paid because of their extra accountability and responsibility why don't their heads roll when things go pear-shaped?

Focus

"Focus on going forward to the next level", means concentrate on improving our trading position. It means much as it does in everyday use only it is used much more in managerese than in day to day conversation.

Demonstrably

Demonstrating-ably?

Eyeballs on the screen

Don't take your eyes off the Powerpoint presentation.

Empowerment

A Management wank word which managers attribute to the cappos who are in charge of restructuring and selling out their work buddies.

Don't beat around the bush

They don't really mean this either, the last thing they want is for you to speak plainly unless you've something nice to say of course.

Fallback position

When it all goes wrong this is where you will be, up shit creek without a paddle.

Back on track

When they believe that the plan is up and running again.

Confidence in the future

Implying that there's this corporate crystal ball where the powers that be can predict the future and that it will be rosy.

Add/create value

All very well and seeming to mean something but beware when the CEO says he's planning to "add value for the shareholder" it generally involves sackings and tightening up on resources. It seldom means that there will be an increase in the Research and Development budget.

Corporate culture

Not always tied in with the reality of the work environment, more a Disney approach to what we think of ourselves.

Dial down

Not quite the thing to speak of projects being put on hold or cancelled, they are simply 'dialled down'.

Develop

Not so popular any more, has largely been superceded by the fuzzier term 'evolve'.

Engaged

Such an interesting term. You can engage the enemy, you can engage your staff to do something for the company, you can engage another prior to marriage. Its very vagueness is so useful in Managerese.

Exciting

The way this is used in the corporate world, a rank and file should be afraid, very afraid. It more than likely means restructures and layoffs with the exception of the Managers of course.

Facilitate

This has come to have broader and broader meaning, it's used to mean 'make easier' but now it equates to 'provide' or 'supply' 'put in place'.

Goal

Cunningly, this has a jaunty sporting feel about it and so suggests something more positive than a military term might.

Paradigm shift

This term epitomises managerese. There are many who sit around the boardroom with only a very vague idea as to what this alludes to but are too shame-faced to say 'please explain!' It means that some other bright management theory has taken stranglehold not because it represents an improvement but because its different and justifies there even being a management stratum.

Synergy

Collaboration or symbiosis, it is a great favourite with the managers, flows off the tongue quite easily.

Talk to

One doesn't talk about things any more one 'talks to' them whether they're inanimate or not. "Now our sales executive Peter Piper will talk to the quarterly report".

Synchronise diaries

Any manager worth his or her salt has a diary that they drag around to all the meetings and are caught synchronising their diaries with the other execs. for the next round of meetings.

Resource-constrained

Short of time, money and staff, in other words running a very lean operation.

Ramping

"We are ramping for a release next quarter" means we are getting ready.

Process

Even though it means much the same as everyday use, it is used very very often in managerese. "Our goal is to focus on process"; "we must review the way we are operating and whether it is efficient"; "we must implement a process for dealing more effectively with the customer"; "we need to find a scheme for interfacing better with the customer."

On the same page

"Are we all on the same page?" Have we all got the same idea in mind?

Outside the box

Even though this term is a favourite of the managers as it suggests they are creative, they really don't want to employ or encourage anyone whose ideas are too far outside the box.

Leverage

In ordinary English this is a noun meaning this is what you possess with a big enough lever, however in managerese it's a verb. "We must leverage our existing resources", take advantage of what we already have.

Mission critical

"We implement mission critical solutions that change the dynamics of the 24/7 infrastructure space". We make computer stuff that needs to run all the time and would be disastrous if they didn't, and we are way ahead of our opposition.

Incentivise

Another of those annoying verbifications of a noun. "We must incentivise individual contributors to adopt a can-do attitude".

Triple bottom line

Here's a classic—this is the evolution into a triumvirate of what used to be called the "bottom line". Now we have social, environmental and financial capital, but with these three the financial is still the bottom line!

Evangelising

A reorganisation announcement by Marconi's EMAA (Europe, Middle East, Africa and Australasia) division

'The benefit of having dedicated subject matter experts who are able to evangelise the attributes and business imperatives of their products is starting to bear fruit.'

Employee Benefits—Guidelines

Dress Code:
It is advised that you come to work dressed according to your salary. If we see you wearing $350 Prada sneakers and carrying a $600 Gucci bag, we assume you are doing well financially and

therefore you do not need a raise. If you dress poorly, you need to learn to manage your money better, so that you may buy nicer clothes and therefore you do not need a raise. If you dress in-between, you are right where you need to be and therefore you do not need a raise.

Sick Days:
We will no longer accept a doctor statement as proof of sickness. If you are able to go to the doctor, you are able to come to work.

Surgery:
Operations are now banned. As long as you are an employee here, you need all your organs. You should not consider removing anything. We hired you intact. To have something removed constitutes a breach of employment.

Personal Days:
Each employee will receive 104 personal days a year. They are called Saturday & Sunday.

Vacation Days:
All employees will take their vacation at the same time, these days are Jan 1, April 25 and Dec 25.

Bereavement Leave:
This is no excuse for missing work. There is nothing you can do for dead friends, relatives or co-workers. Every effort should be made to have non-employees attend to the arrangements. In rare cases where employee involvement is necessary, the funeral should be scheduled in the late afternoon. We will be glad to allow you to work through your lunch hour and subsequently leave one hour early, provided your share of the work is done.

Absence due to your own death:
This will be accepted as an excuse. However, we require at least two weeks notice as it is your duty to train your own replacement.

Restroom use:
Entirely too much time is being spent in the restroom. In the future, we will follow the practice of going in alphabetical order.

For instance, all employees whose names begin with 'A' will go from 8:00 to 8:20, Employees whose names begin with 'B' will go from 8:20 to 8:40 and so on. If you're unable to go at your allotted time, it will be necessary to wait until the next day when your turn comes again. In extreme emergencies, employees may swap their time with a co-worker. Both employees' supervisors must approve this exchange in writing and in advance of the need. In addition, there is now a strict three minute time limit in the stalls. At the end of three minutes, an alarm will sound, the toilet paper roll will retract, the stall door will open and a picture will be taken. After your second offence, your picture will be posted on the company bulletin board under the "Chronic Offenders" category.

Lunch Break:
Skinny people get 30 minutes for lunch as they need to eat more so that they can look healthy. Normal size people get 15 minutes for lunch to get a balanced meal to maintain their average figure. Fat people get 5 minutes for lunch, because that's all the time needed to drink a Slim Fast and take a diet pill.

Thank you for your loyalty to our company. We are here to provide a positive employment experience. Therefore, all questions, comments, concerns, complaints, frustrations, irritations, aggravations, insinuations, allegations, accusations, contemplations, consternation and input should be directed elsewhere.

Have a nice week.
The Management

Gobbledygook

'The geometric foundation of the design is based upon a circular form, which makes reference to the Institution's global perspective and international reputation in teaching and research. The typographic elements demonstrate a hierarchy which promotes the importance of the location within the nomenclature. The group of circles represents the incremental growth of knowledge and experience and the progressive development of the University as an educational leader. This thematic device continues through to the linear band on the right of the Shield of Arms and describes the cyclical movement of time, indicating progression and new directions.'

University of Dundee for design rationale of Corporate identity.

Worker dead at desk for 5 days

Bosses of a publishing firm are trying to work out why no one noticed that one of their employees had been sitting dead at his desk for FIVE DAYS before anyone asked if he was feeling okay. George Turklebaum, 51, who had been employed as a proof-reader at a New York firm for 30 years, had a heart attack in the open-plan office he shared with 23 other workers. He quietly passed away on Monday, but nobody noticed until Saturday morning when an office cleaner asked why he was still working during the weekend. His boss Elliot Wachiaski said "George was always the first guy in each morning and the last to leave at night, so no one found it unusual that he was in the same position all that time and didn't say anything. "He was always absorbed in his work and kept much to himself." A post mortem examination revealed that he had been dead for five days after suffering a coronary. Ironically, George was proof reading manuscripts of medical textbooks when he died. You may want to give your co-workers a nudge occasionally.

And the moral of the story:

Don't work too hard. Nobody notices anyway.

De-jobbed

If lawyers are disbarred and clergymen defrocked, doesn't it follow that electricians can be delighted, musicians denoted, cowboys deranged, spies decoded, models deposed and dry cleaners depressed? Laundry workers could decrease, eventually becoming depressed and depleted!

Bed makers will be debunked, sign painters designed, baseball players will be debased, landscapers will be deflowered, bulldozer operators will be degraded, organ donors will be delivered, software engineers will be detested, the BVD company will be debriefed, and even musical composers will eventually decompose. On a more positive note though, perhaps we can hope politicians will be devoted.

Euphemisms for layoffs and firings

The words employers use to get rid of staff, are very numerous, and creative after all, it doesn't sound so bad if you're just being "cashiered" or "decruited" now does it?

Boomerang

1. An employee who leaves through one door as an employee of the company and returns as a consultant, often on a better hourly rate and for fewer hours. No tenure, however.
2. An employee who's laid off but rehired later, because they still need the skills.

Brightsizing

Corporate downsizing in which the brightest workers are let go. This happens when a company lays off those workers with the least seniority, but it's those young workers who are often the best trained and educated.

Capsizing

Downsizing a workforce to the point where the company goes under.

Career Change Opportunity
A non-voluntary one. Companies are becoming quite creative at coining these euphemisms. Other examples include involuntary separation from payroll, decruitment, repositioning, reshaping, and focused reduction.

Cashier
To fire an employee.

Chain Saw Consultant
A consultant who has the job of chopping staff numbers, thus leaving the hands of the top executives unsullied.

Consolidation
Usually involving the firing of employees or the reduction of services and plant.

Corporate Anorexia
When a business becomes so fearful of not being lean that it cuts staff and costs to the point that it's running on empty and about to roll over and die anyway.

Cost containment
Once again one does not need to employ much imagination, fire the employees and reduce services to the customer.

Decruitment
The antonym to recruitment, yes you guessed it, more layoffs.

Dehire
The firing of employees "we were forced to dehire the sales team for Angaston".

Downaging
As it sounds, companies who want to lower the average age of their employees by getting rid of the older ones or actively only recruiting the young guns. So much for the "ageless employee".

Dumbsizing
Taking the downsizing of staff to the point of idiocy where it is no longer efficient or effective or profitable.

Exit Memo
This is the farewell memo written to other employees of the company when the author is about to exit stage left.

Ghost Work
This is the work that still needs to be done after a series of layoffs and is usually picked up by remaining staff, however it proves bad for morale because they may have already had big workloads, and the smell of fear is still thick.

Inshoring
Gaining local jobs when the offshore boys expand their business enterprises, very capricious however as they may pull out at any time.

Jettison Employees
Like sandbags off a hot air balloon, the workers are thrown out into the world of the jobless.

Layoff Lust
The rampant desire to be laid off from one's job "Pick me! Pick me!".

Leaner
Once having laid off those employees and gotten rid of that plant, the remaining staff are expected to achieve the same results with much less.

Nearshoring
Restructuring a company's workforce to move jobs to a nearby and cheaper employment option.

Offshoreable
The feasibility of being moved to another country, especially to reduce costs; capable of being performed by a person in another country, especially at a lower wage or salary.

Pare Down
No, not toenails or horse's hooves, but employees and the resources needed to function.

Payroll Orphans
Employees who've been severed from their umbilical pay supply.

Pink Slip Party
In order to get into this party you must recently have been laid off work (particularly popular with the dot.com industry). A form of commiseration and networking.

Presenteeism
Having to show up for work even when sick or stressed and not feeling at all productive. Even doing overtime when there is really nothing to do, for fear of being found wanting.

Ramping Down An Operation
Targeting a part of the company's structure and sacking employees or reducing services or plant.

Regime Change
Tongue-in-cheek irony as to a change in leadership be it in business, politics or sport.

RIF
A take on Rest in Peace, only the passing over in this instance is from employment to unemployment.

Rightshoring
Restructuring a company's workforce to find the optimum mix of jobs performed locally and jobs moved to foreign countries. Which demi-god is to get this mix just right? Must be one of the executives.

Rightsizing
Downsizing a company's workforce to the point where the number of employees remaining is deemed to be "right" for the company's current condition.

Sacrifice
"Some sacrifice is needed to improve profit". Guess whose sacrifice? Why the usual suspects, the employees who get laid off and the plant reduction etc.

Smartsizing
Getting rid of the supposed deadwood so you are left with only the best and brightest.

Surplused
"The firm surplused several employees" i.e. deemed them unnecessary to the continued working of the company.

Uninstalled
A euphemism for being ejected from the company.

Upstaff
Sometimes when they realize they might have taken the layoffs too far, the managers go through a recruiting drive to start adding employees again. Considering the cost of layoff packages and the recruitment and induction costs of new employees, it is not the most efficient way to go about things.

Warm chair attrition
Workplace productivity lost by employees who dislike their jobs, whose hearts are simply not in it, and are biding their time until something better comes along. Contract workers often spend a good deal of their time into the last months of their contract casting around for other opportunities.

Worklessness
The rather hopeless condition of being unemployed stretching far into the future.

Consultant or prostitute?

1. You work very odd hours.
2. You are paid a lot of money to keep your client happy.
3. You are paid well but your pimp gets most of the money.
4. You spend a majority of your time in a hotel room.
5. You charge by the hour but your time can be extended.
6. You are not proud of what you do.
7. Creating fantasies for your clients is rewarded.
8. It's difficult to have a family.
9. You have no job satisfaction.
10. If a client beats you up, the pimp just sends you to another client.
11. You are embarrassed to tell people what you do for a living.
12. People ask you, "What do you do?" and you can't explain it.
13. Your client pays for your hotel room plus your hourly rate.
14. Your client always wants to know how much you charge and what they get for the money.
15. Your pimp drives nice cars like Mercedes or Jaguars.
16. You know the pimp is charging more than you are worth but if the client is foolish enough to pay it's not your problem.
17. When you leave to go see a client, you look great, but return looking like hell (compare your appearance on Monday AM to Friday PM).
18. You are rated on your "performance" in an excruciating ordeal.
19. Even though you might get paid the big bucks, it's the client who walks away smiling.
20. The client always thinks your "cut" of your billing rate is higher than it actually is, and in turn, expects miracles from you.
21. When you deduct your "take" from your billing rate, you constantly wonder if you could get a better deal with another pimp.

Team Building

How many of you in Corporate La-la Land have heard the tired old expression "when you ASSUME you make an ASS out of you and ME" or "there is no I in TEAM" when attending a team-building seminar? Well there are ways to expand on the flimsiness of this kind of propaganda, by using the power of the anagram to make fun of the jargon used so often by managers, mission statements and corporate plans. You will no doubt warm to the theme and have fun adding some of your own.

When you **enhance**, you give a **hen acne**.

When you use **facilitate**, you put a **tail** on your **face**.

When you **customise**, you make a **stoic** out of **me**.

When you **innovate**, you speak in a **vain tone**.

When you talk of **paradigm shifts**, I want to put my **fist** in your **diaphragm.**

When you **disseminate**, you take the **inmate's side**.

When you use **catalysts for change**, you play **tag** with the **flycatcher's ass.**

When you are **market-driven**, you should be sent as an **errant** to **Kiev**.

When you use **world's best practice**, you should give the **terrestrial** a **bow**.

When you use **cutting edge**, you should win the **dunce's egg**.

When you say **methods of empowerment**, you should be put in the pen with a **hot-tempered sow**.

When you tell us it's **economically sound**, we draw the **conclusion** that you can **yodel**.

When you use **damage limitation**, you could **maim** your **genitalia**.

When you use **in the final analysis**, what you **say** is **infantile**.

When you talk of **continuous improvement**, you bring out the **contemptuous** side of **men**.

When you say **make no mistake about it**, you **abominate** and **mutate**.

When you talk of **absolute certainty**, you **articulate** with a crooked **bent**.

When you mouth **I hear what you're saying**, it's pure **generosity** to permit you an **airway**.

When you say **do more with less**, you should give a **worthless demo**.

When you intone **work smarter not harder**, you should be declared a **dank sort of earthworm**.

When you talk of **fidicuary capitalism**, you perpetrate a **fraud** against **simplicity**.

If you talk of **strategic philanthropy**, you've lost your **hypothetical grip**.

When you talk of **rat-race equilibrium**, you might **rile** a **bureaucrat**.

When you say **the fact of the matter is**, you leave an **aftertaste of moth**.

When you start with **to be perfectly honest**, I just know I'm going to be hearing some **fence post theory**.

When you plan to **address the issue**, I expect that **distress** is **due**.

When you plan a **performance appraisal**, the poor staff member can expect some **impersonal crap**.

And lastly …

There is no I in **Team**

There is no I in **Team**, but there's no **we** or **us** either

There is no I in **Team**, but there is a kind of **me**

There is no I in **Team**, but there is an I in **Cooperation** and **Collaboration.**

Memo to all staff

Due to the current financial situation caused by the slow down of economy in US since last Christmas, Management has decided to implement a scheme to put workers of 40 years of age on early retirement. This scheme will be known as RAPE (Retire Aged People Early).

Persons selected to be RAPED can apply to management to be eligible for the SHAFT scheme (Special Help After Forced Termination).

Persons who have been RAPED and SHAFTED will be reviewed under the SCREW scheme (Scheme Covering Retired Early Workers).

A person may be RAPED once, SHAFTED twice and SCREWED as many times as Management deems appropriate.

Persons who have been RAPED can only get AIDS (Additional Income for Dependants of Spouse) or HERPES (Half Earnings for Retired Personnel Early Severance). Obviously persons who have AIDS or HERPES will not be SHAFTED or SCREWED any further by management.

Persons staying on will receive as much SHIT (Special High Intensity Training) as possible. Management has always prided itself on the amount of SHIT it gives employees. Should you feel that you do not receive enough SHIT, please bring to the attention of your Supervisor. They have been trained to give you all the SHIT you can handle.

Sincerely,
The Management

Achieving More

We have all been to those meetings where someone wants over 100%. Here's to achieving 103%. Here's a little math that might prove helpful in the future! If...

A	1	O	15
B	2	P	16
C	3	Q	17
D	4	R	18
E	5	S	19
F	6	T	20
G	7	U	21
H	8	V	22
I	9	W	23
J	10	X	24
K	11	Y	25
L	12	Z	26
M	13		
N	14		

Then...

H A R D W O R K
8 1 18 4 23 15 18 11 = 98 % Only

K N O W L E D G E
11 14 15 23 12 5 4 7 5 = 96 % Only

But...

A T T I T U D E
1 20 20 9 20 21 4 5 = 100 %

However...
B U L L S H I T
2 21 12 12 19 8 9 20 = 103%

The danger of switching jobs

A passenger in a taxi tapped the driver on the shoulder to ask him something. The driver screamed, lost control of the cab, nearly hit a bus, drove up over the curb and stopped just inches from a large plate glass window. For a few moments everything was silent in the cab, then the driver said, "Please, don't ever do that again. You scared the daylights out of me." The passenger, who was also frightened, apologised and said he didn't realize that a tap on the shoulder could frighten him so much, to which the driver replied, "I'm sorry, it's really not your fault at all. Today is my first day driving a cab. I have been driving a hearse for the last 25 years."

Balls and the corporate ladder

After a two-year study, the National Science Foundation announced the following results on the Working male's recreational preferences:

1. The sport of choice for unemployed or incarcerated people is: basketball
2. The sport of choice for maintenance-level employees is: bowling.
3. The sport of choice for blue-collar workers is: football.
4. The sport of choice for supervisors is: baseball.
5. The sport of choice for middle management is: tennis.
6. The sport of choice for corporate officers is: golf.

Conclusion:
The higher you rise in the corporate structure, the smaller your balls become.

Always give 100% at work:

12% on Monday
23% on Tuesday
40% on Wednesday
20% on Thursday
5% on Fridays

"So much of what we call management consists in making it difficult for people to work."

Peter F Drucker

Ads, Fads and Scams

"Advertising may be described as the science of arresting human intelligence long enough to get money from it."

Stephen B. Leacock

"Advertising is the art of convincing people to spend money they don't have for something they don't need."

Will Rogers

Advertising

How does what's out there in the stores dovetail with what we want, what we absolutely have to own?

How do fashions change? One year, women's fashion dictates fabrics all flowing and sensuous, the next year the clothing is a line of figure-hugging straitjackets. The wildebeest-followers-of-fashion dart across the s-veldt of fashion history zigging this way and zagging that way. It even overrides the reality that most of our figures are not suited to the whims of fashion.

Well, we are exposed to what amounts to brainwashing. With the influence of high-profile models and clever campaigns we are convinced they are cool and we just have to own them.

This is how it works. Trend setters (electronic whiz kids, fashion designers, toy manufacturers) design new things they believe will be good for us. Then they use marketing specialists to persuade us that we need these things, which sparks our desire, a compelling desire "I must have one of those or two perhaps" and the products start flying off the shelves.

So the equation is:

New Products/Services + Marketing =Desire=Demand=Supply=Sales

The arbiters of fashion and style and the acceptable let us know what's in; what's out; what's cool; what's crap; what's hot and what's not. Every day we are persuaded we need to buy new things and rid ourselves of the "old".

Why for instance do we ever get rid of those appliances, cars and homes where everything is still working wonderfully well? Not that it's wrong to buy new things. What the problem here is that you are convinced you need them. Yes if you want something because you think it would be fun, fine; but not if you allow someone to make you feel bad because you didn't make the purchase.

Marketers' stock-in-trade is to keeping us wanting things, the thirst that can't be quenched. Once having realized this we can make informed decisions about how we spend our money or even the wisdom of going into debt over something we may not need.

So many purchases are thrown away even before their packaging gets to the dump. Clothes sit in wardrobes having been worn only once or not at all.

So you think you're immune to all that advertising hype and pizzazz—the way to tell if that's true is to answer these questions and if you say "yes" to even one of them you may be susceptible.

- Have you ever wanted to throw out all the clothes you have from the last season and completely start to build your wardrobe of clothes again?
- Would you like to move in and live permanently in a hardware store?
- Have you ever wanted to chuck out all your existing furniture and start all over again with the décor after going to a furniture store?

- Do you find yourself browsing the new tools section of the hardware store even though the tools you have don't get used?
- Are you tempted to buy a new TV or VCR just because they're having a sale even though the ones you have are working perfectly?
- Do you go weak at the knees inside certain curio shops or gourmet kitchens because you just love everything in there and want to buy all of it?
- Do stationery and office supplies stores leave you feeling weak with desire?
- Do you find yourself looking longingly in the jeweller's window at the watches and bracelets even though you already have an elegant sufficiency?

By being aware that your desires and continual 'want, want, want' is being manipulated by powerful forces, you can take control and resist the unceasing temptations, moving from automatic pilot to being able to make informed choices.

Try something as simple as saying before any purchase "do I really need this? Will I still need it and have a use for it in a year's/a month's/a day's time?"

Ad Speak

Here are some newly coined terms which capture a little of the spirit of our times. Note the creep of advertising and commerce into every area of life. For example, in the United States, a couple expecting their first baby put their babe's name up for auction on the Net. Were they prepared for their little one to be a walking billboard for Nike, Coca-Cola, or Benetton?

Ad Creep
Like an out-of-control vine in a feral garden, ads are spreading across non-traditional surfaces such as sides of buildings, cars, bathroom walls.

Advermation
(Advertisement + information) it's an advertisement providing detailed information about the product in question.

Advertecture
Ads painted as murals onto walls of buildings.

Advertorial
This is an ad disguised as editorial content.

Badge Item
Some signifying item, a trinket or piece of clothing a person wears to proclaim their personality.

Billboard Liberation
Modification of the billboard or other ads that changes the message of the ad.

Brandalism
(Brand + vandalism) branding's way of defacing public space, the logos and corporate ads writ large.

Brand Name Dropping
Using every opportunity to mention the names of the good and services one owns.

Culture Jamming
Anti-consumer campaign that uses mass media to convey their message.

Commercial Creep
When the zoning for the residential areas is gradually encroached upon by the commercial district.

Drip Marketing
This describes a direct marketing ploy which involves sending off several promotional pieces over time to a subset of sales leads.

Entertoyment
The massive tie-in campaigns that cover release of blockbusters such as Star Wars, Toy Story and Spiderman, toys galore! And the whole ad strategy depending on the kids who go to these then nag their parents about the action figure.

Fictomercial
Product placement a company pays for in a work of fiction where the product can feature.

Guerilla Marketing
A slightly feral marketing campaign using non-traditional tactics and locations, often flouting local laws and statutes.

Kidfluence
Obvious and covert ways that kids have of influencing their parent's purchases.

Marketecture
1. Just like apartments that get sold off from the plan, this is new computer architecture getting the hard sell even though it doesn't even exist yet.

2. A marketing campaign's structure or design.

Nag Factor
There's an axiom, "the element in any system with the most flexibility wields the most power". A child, not conditioned yet to follow any ethical laws, uses its powers of manipulation both direct "Mum, mum, mum, mum" and covert "Johnny Appleseed brought this really cool velocaraptor to school, I've lost all my friends—they want to play with Johnny and not me. Waaaaaah!" The companies advertising toys that children must, must, must have know this very well. It is also known that children have a problem drawing the line between reality and unreality. So when someone interrupts a cartoon to tell them to go out and get Wizzlefuzzle and get it now, they are out of their beanbags and into the kitchen to tell the parents they want it now, now, now! See 'pester power' and 'kidfluence'.

Neuromarketing
Doing a neurological study of a person's responses and mental state when being exposed to the marketing message.

Pesterpower
The awesome power children possess to coerce their parents into buying things they'd rather not buy and doing things they'd rather not do.

Pollution on a stick
A rather derogatory term for billboards.

Proletarian Drift
The trend of products which were once only procured by the upper classes becoming popular with the working class; the tendency for new elements to become appealing eventually to the lowest common denominator.

Promo-tainment
Promotion wearing the guise of entertainment.

Splurchandising
Deliberately setting up the merchandise to lead to a splurge of impulse purchasing.

Squeeze-and-Tease
Squashing a TV show's credits into about a third of the screen in order to advertise upcoming shows.

Undercover Marketing
Actors marketing products in a real-life setting while posing as regular people.

Snob Effect
Wanting to purchase something for the sole reason that it is extremely expensive or rare; the way demand increases proportionately with the price of an item and the perception that it confers social status to the consumer.

Truth in Advertising?

The following is an ad from a real-life newspaper that appeared four days in a row, the last three hopelessly trying to correct the first day's mistake.

Monday
For sale: R.D. Jones has one sewing machine for sale. Phone 948-0707 after 7 P.M. and ask for Mrs. Kelly who lives with him cheap.

Tuesday
Notice: We regret having erred in R.D. Jones' ad yesterday. It should have read "One sewing machine for sale cheap. Phone 948-0707 and ask for Mrs. Kelly, who lives with him after 7 P.M."

Wednesday
Notice: R.D. Jones has informed us that he has received several annoying telephone calls because of the error we made in the classified ad yesterday. The ad stands correct as follows: "For sale: R.D. Jones has one sewing machine for sale. Cheap. Phone 948-0707 after 7 P.M. and ask for Mrs. Kelly who lives with him."

Thursday
Notice: I, R.D. Jones, have no sewing machine for sale. I smashed it. Don't call 948-0707 as I have had the phone disconnected. I have not been carrying on with Mrs. Kelly. Until yesterday she was my housekeeper but she quit!

What's in a Name, Nom, Nombre, Naam?

Yes it's true that advertising can be very persuasive but sometimes its effectiveness is lost in translation. Here are some examples:

When the Pope was coming to Miami, a T-shirt company thought it would promote his visit however they made a mistake – instead of "I saw the Pope **(el Papa)**" the shirts read "I saw the potato" **(la papa).**

Turn it loose
Coors campaign in Spain read as "suffer from diarrhoea".

Nothing sucks like an Electrolux
Was the Scandinavian Electrolux campaign they launched in the US.

Mist Stick
A curling iron introduced by Clairol into Germany found that "mist" is slang for manure.

Salem Feeling Free
was Salem cigarette's slogan introduced into the Japanese market – translates as "When smoking Salem you will feel so refreshed that your mind seems to be empty".

Cue
was a new line of toothpaste that Colgate introduced into France before they realized that Cue is the name for a notorious porn magazine.

Schweppes
Tonic Water campaign didn't go down too well in Italy, it translated as "Schweppes Toilet Water".

In Chinese "Come alive with the **Pepsi Generation**" translates to "Pepsi brings your ancestors back from the grave".

"It won't leak in your pocket and embarrass you"
Was Parker Pen's campaign slogan for the leak-proof ballpoint pen intended for the Mexican market, one problem, "embarazar" the word they used for embarrass means impregnate so the ad read **"It won't leak in your pocket and make you pregnant"**.

Marketing analogies

This is an explanatory exercise about marketing with women as the target audience.

Direct Marketing
You see a handsome guy at a party. You go up to him and say, "I'm fantastic in bed."

Advertising
You're at a party with a bunch of friends and see a handsome guy. One of your friends goes up to him and, pointing at you, says, "She's fantastic in bed."

Telemarketing
You see a handsome guy at a party. You go up to him and get his telephone number. The next day you call and say, "Hi, I'm fantastic in bed."

Public Relations
You're at a party and see a handsome guy. You get up and straighten your dress. You walk up to him and pour him a drink. You say, "May I," and reach up to straighten his tie brushing your breast lightly against his arm, and then say, "By the way, I'm fantastic in bed."

Brand Recognition
You're at a party and see a handsome guy. He walks up to you and says, "I hear you're fantastic in bed."

Sales Rep
You're at a party and see a handsome guy. You talk him into going home with your friend.

Tech Support
Your friend can't satisfy him so he calls you.

Spam
You're on your way to a party when you realize that there could be handsome men in all these houses you're passing. So you climb

onto the roof of one situated toward the centre and shout at the top of your lungs, "I'm fantastic in bed!"

Doctors of Spin

We read Him here, we hear Her there,
We chase those true lies everywhere,
Whispering scribe of the story we're in,
That devilish, dastardly Doctor of Spin!

Jack Robertson

Spin

Spin was originally an acronym for "significant progress in the news" and first started being used in the mid-1980s. The public relations specialists for Strategic Defence Institute in the US were having to defend SDI which was receiving some heavy criticism about being impractical, "spin" declared the news releases announcing steady progress.

The manager and the organisation or corporation have this tendency to wrap their behaviours in pretty sounding but vacuous motherhood statements. They state that their chief focus is the customer or client but we know that profitability is the "bottom line". And they state how much they value their staff but we know from the speed at which they shed jobs, this is clearly not a "Core Belief".

The world of public relations also seeks to assuage its conscience with codes of ethical conduct.

Those who coin the words would have you believe that public relations practitioners are in the business of promoting "honesty, accuracy, integrity and truth" and whereas these words and sentiments are truly inspirational, it totally ignores what the core business of public relations is, namely the advocacy and dissemination of the partisan viewpoints of those who engage their services, for the benefit of those who engage their services; the maximisation of advantage for those who engage their services and any assistance provided in making their competitors seem less able through smear campaigns or other tools is seen as fair game.

All is fair in war and public relations.

There are situations of course where it is in the interest of the 'candidate' to be open and honest and, where that brief is not in conflict with the protection of his or her interests, the PR person will utilise this particular advantage to the max.

However it is more realistic to say that very often it is in the client's interest that certain facts never see the light of day, and if they do make the tabloids, the PR person works strenuously with every resource at hand to minimise the impact on that client's credibility and reputation and suitability for office. It's called 'crisis avoidance' and 'damage control'.

The client needn't be a person, it can be a company. Where the company is perceived as the victim then of course it is in the interest of the PR to utilise the transparency argument, but where the corporation is quite noticeably at fault e.g. the Exxon Valdiz where a rather large oil spill was hard to cover up or negate, then it's a matter of employing a very different tack.

When does describing a "nearly empty" bottle as "almost full" go from extreme optimism to a flagrant distortion of the truth? They in the business like to call it "focused messaging" but in plain language that means a highly selective presentation of information. Which may serve the clients' interest very well but is of no use to Joe Public.

This would not be such a problem if there was an admission by the Public Relations firms, the managers, the politicians that they are self-serving and stop with the BS about caring for humanity, the environment and ethics such as honesty. If the truth is so easily manipulated into all kinds of shapes, when does it cease to be true?

Public Relations, When Disaster Strikes

Public relations is a way of making whatever individual or organization look "good" no matter what, despite any eventuality or disaster, scandal, acts of God, a fall in the Stock Exchange, murder you name it.

Here's a list of the possible disasters that may befall:

Acts of God
The popular press often characterise such things as tsunamis and earthquakes as PR disasters for tourist destinations and whole countries. Which of course is true, only the public is more likely to have largesse about things God has a hand in.

Business Operations
Here's where some corporate event or activity impacts adversely on the stakeholder groups. For instance, when Coca-Cola and Pepsi were having to defend themselves in India against allegations that their soft drinks contained unacceptable levels of toxins. From a PR viewpoint, this was not handled well as instead of calming matters down, both companies managed to fan the flames of discontent.

Corporate Moves
When there is a big change afoot as in times of takeovers, acquisitions and mergers it can become the portal for scandal or dissatisfaction. For example, when a PR man used his insider knowledge to trade in stock and was found out.

Legalities
Debate in court over a case which is then reported by the media. The McDonalds McLibel case was a notorious instance of this, the media watchers labelled it 'the world's biggest corporate PR disaster'.

Rumours
When it comes to brand reputation and brand credibility, gossip can be extremely damaging. Procter & Gamble found this out when malicious rumours of Satanism circulated. It was in part

propagated by a P&G competitor but it dogged the company for decades and caused the company to invest in a complete worldwide logo redesign and much work done by PR firms to turn it around.

Staff

An instance happened at the time of the 9/11 towers debacle. Starbucks staff working close to Ground Zero were charging rescue workers for bottled water they were using to treat victims with. When word got out about this seeming heartlessness the publicity was extremely damaging to Starbucks.

Scandal

Sex and financial carry-ons usually guarantee there'll be an interest from the media. A recent example is Shane Warne, the famous Australian spin bowler whose sexual escapades led to sponsors removing their accreditation.

Disaster – Hard to contain

From the point of view of anyone in PR it must seem that the profession never learns by its mistakes and some are incredibly monumental, however there are certain incendiaries that are very hard to contain. The mix of malpractice (by clients and PR), misjudgement (by PR people not being able to read the exact impact of the latest event) and then of course the media's insatiable appetite for stories which will impact negatively on anyone. The media relies on "disaster editorial content".

Advertising Claims

Advertisers know that a well designed ad campaign has dramatic effects. Despite the fact that the campaigns can be laughed at, belittled and all but ignored, they still have an effect.

The very ones the ad men rub their hands in glee about are the audience who believe ads are harmless and they are immune from such nonsense. Whereas advertising can be studied in detail to uncover the psychological hooks to rope in the unwary, probably the best way to analyse them is to look at the language of the advertising claim.

The "claim" is the verbal or print part of the ad making some claim of superiority for the product in question. Some claims are boldfaced lies, some actually tell you the truth about a superior product but most are neither. They teeter like a tightrope walker between truth and falsehood by the crafty choice of words.

Here are the kinds of claims advertisers make:

1. We're different and unique

The assumption here is that because the product is purportedly unique, it must then follow that it is superior to other products.

Examples:

"There's no shampoo like it"

"The Shitatsu is like nobody else's car"

"Any way you look at it, there's nothing else like it"

2. Water is wet

The trick here is that the claim they make about the product holds true for any comparable product. It's usually made in the form of a statement, but confers no advantage on the advertised product over its competition.

Examples:

"Maxi-Lash greatly increases the diameter of each lash"

"Shteingoot, the natural beer" It's made from grain and water, as are other beers.

"Aromaz smells different on everyone" And so do many other perfumes.

3. Compliment the consumer

Flattery is weaving its charm here, boosting the ego of the consumer.

Examples:

"The lady has great taste"

"Oh baby, have you come a long way!"

"You pride yourself on keeping your family safe ..."

4. So what?

The claim may be true but gives no real advantage to the product, the careful reader will react with a "so what?"

"VitaVix has twice the magnesium of ordinary supplements"
However is twice the dose a benefit to health?

"Bonzo Soup has not two but three special stocks"
Does that improve the taste?

"Cheezsciz is powerful enough to cut through stone"
But this product is only meant to cut cheese.

5. Rhetorical question

A question is pitched to the audience and evokes an answer which is favourable to the product. Watch for "shouldn'ts" and "wouldn'ts" and such.

Examples:

"Shouldn't you be treating your family to a UBUTE BBQ this summer?"

"DreamBreeze, wouldn't your body love to sink into this mattress every night?"

"ZaggenWagon, shouldn't all families be enjoying the luxury of this people mover?"

6. Endorsement or Testimonial

A celebrity female with oodles of long flowing locks appears in a shampoo ad, or else an authority e.g. dentist for toothpaste or toothbrushes. Sometimes they claim they use it themselves but watch carefully because very often they don't. Testimonials are a very powerful technique.

Examples:

"Darling, why don't you offer them a Shlibovitz Vodka? Most of my best friends love that drink" Zsa Zsa Gabor

"Dentists endorse BLANCO as the recommended toothpaste"
With the figure brushing his teeth shown from the back and no names given.

"Matsubishu is the best small car in the Southern Hemisphere"
This claim is used but may only be a quote taken from a car magazine.

7. Scientific or Statistical

Usually some kind of scientific testing is used, or statistical figures or impressive chemical ingredients.

"WakeUpFresh, 35% more nutrition"

"Ostofree, created by a scientist who suffers from arthritis"

"BreathEaze contains a special ingredient, polyvolywoly"

8. Vague

It's just not clear what the claim is and often overlaps with others. Key to identifying this kind of technique is that the words are flamboyant but meaningless. Also they use subjective and emotive opinions which cannot be verified.

"Pollygobblers are so much fun, they look good, smell good and taste good"

"Take one sip and you'll feel like you're sitting in a piazza in Florence"

"Kubanka tastes good like a good cigar should"

9. Unfinished

When the ad claims the product is better, faster, tastier but doesn't finish by telling you what it's comparing.

"CondoBondo 300% stickier"

"Sharziq gives you more"

"Fandangle goes further every time"

10. Weasel

Weasel words are the kind that suck the meaning out of the accompanying word or words just as weasels suck the goodness out of eggs by taking out the inside and leaving the shell. Some common weasely words are "helps"; "like" used in the comparative sense, "virtual or virtually"; "fortified" or "enriched".

"Helps contain hair loss symptoms with regular use"
It is not claiming to stop hair loss only weaseling the suggestion in.

"Leaves your windows virtually streak-free" Our minds have learned to tune out the qualifying weasel words, but virtually can mean 'nearly' which doesn't mean streak 'free.'

"Only half the price of many carpet cleaners" Here the weasel is "many". It's meant to imply that the cleaner is cheap.

Fads

Synonyms for **Fad**: craze; fashion; furore; mode; rage; style; trend; vogue.

Fad in other languages

French: vogue
German: tick, marotte
Dutch: rage, lievelingsidee
Italian: moda, voga, mania
Portuguese: moda, passageira
Spanish: moda, furor, novedad

"Fads are the kiss of death.
When the fad goes away, you go with it".

Conway Twitty

"Nobody creates a fad.
It just happens.
People love going along with the idea of a beautiful pig.
It's like a conspiracy."

Jim Henson talking about Miss Piggy

Thought to have been derived originally from fid fad, a fussy person, or fiddle-faddle, the fad is a following for a product or regime or fashion that climbs very rapidly to frenzied proportions and is fuelled nowadays by the opportunistic marketplace. It can last for weeks or years, however it does eventually have a cooling off and sometimes disappears into obscurity with a speed that rivals the speed with which it became famous.
Pokemon cards were such an addictive fad some of the schools had to ban bringing the cards to school and trading them, such a distraction was it causing to school life.

Some terms which might explain the bizarre fad phenomenon are:

Bandwagon Effect
People are often motivated to do things because a lot of other people are doing the same thing.

Herd instinct
We act like herd animals, the wildebeest, the lemmings too sometimes. The groupthink mentality that can protect but can also cause disasters when the masses throw themselves off the cliff.

Sheeple
Combining 'sheep' and 'people' this is a term of disparagement. The gullibility factor in human culture where some of us are believed whatever we are told, without employing critical thinking. It's generally used in a political sense.

YTMND
"You're the Man Now Dog", which could apply to the latest hottest fad.

Internet Phenomenon
How the Net can amplify the focus on some product or notion or craze to the point of giving it overnight stardom, however the phenomenon is usually short-lived.

Examples over the last few decades are:

Bungee balls	2003
Cabbage patch dolls	2003
Spongebob Squarepants	2000s
Pokemon	1990s-2000s
Cargo Pantslate	1990s
JNCO -wide legged jeans	1990s
Rubik's Cube	1980s
Designer jeans	1980s
Mood ring	1970s
Pet rocks	1970s
Coonskin caps	1950s
Hula Hoop	1950s
Yo-yo	1930s and 1990s

For the purposes of this book the phenomenon of the fad diet will be explored and diets will also be investigated when looking at scams.

Fad Diets

The weight loss industry is huge across the western world. The reality is that the majority of women and an increasing number of men will go on a diet some time in the course of the year. Some will succeed at taking off the weight but very few; as little as 5 percent will manage to keep the weight off for the long run.

The reason for the dismal failure rate is that so many are looking for a quick-fix. They just find it hard to believe when they live in such sophisticated times with such incredible gadgets and medical miracles being announced daily that something as simple as a weight loss program that works doesn't exist.

So they succumb to ones that are telling them what they believe should be the case. "**Eat all you want and lose weight; no exercise necessary; slap on this patch and you'll have a butt to drool about"** and think that this will lead them to a happier, slimmer, more attractive future.

It's not easy being a fad diet. From nowhere it seems you come like a Haley's Comet streaking across the Diet Sky, all faces upturned to wonder at your glory, all other fad diets eclipsed by your magnificence. You're the talk-of-the-town, every shopping line queue is singing your praises, the hairdressers are full of the chant of diet xxxx, dinner party conversations are dominated with enthusiastic dialogues about you, and your cult followers are spreading the 'bible of diet xxxxx'. You're on TV and in the press and the white coat wearing experts-for-hire are giving a dazzling array of statistics about your success and demonstrating how Rat 12435 lost half its body weight and has gone on to live twice as long as its usual life expectancy of six months.

The next minute the s**t hits the fan and you're branded an irresponsible health risk. A Hollywood child prodigy who grew up to be an Ordinary Joe would know exactly how you feel.

One thing is certain, there is a captive audience that remains a constant and may well be increasing, the "**Thinness Lust**" fuelled by images everywhere of svelte models and size 0 actresses, piled on top of 'body image' issues and low self-esteem.

The entrepreneur who is able to put a new spin on what is a 'thinly' disguised caloric reduction, with gimmicks of "facts" and credible sounding "research" and slick looking testimonials, can with some good marketing seize the day, for a while anyway.

Life Cycle of a Fad Diet

Stage One – Precautionary Optimism

The is-it-for-real phase. It just seems to promise so much that the diet devotee is somewhat cautious and wary.

Stage Two – Giddy Enthusiasm

Everybody who is anybody in the dieting world is on it and it's delivering results. Millions of kilos lost across the face of the known world and it's creating a buzz.

Stage Three – Creeping Disillusionment

Weight loss honeymoon over, loss beginning to slow down and plateau. Dieter asking "how long can I continue with this?"

Stage Four – Diet Has-been

The diet goes down as part of the history of "been there, done that" diets. Either shelved or thrown in the dust bin.

Stage Five – Rebound phase

After having followed the diet for days or weeks, the dieter reverts to 'normal eating', whatever that was. Weight is gained back and the dieter has a choice: blame diet or blame oneself.

However, that same diet devotee can fall foul of the next fad diet to come along, swept away by the frenzied hype and a deep abiding optimism that just like the search for a soul mate, there is a diet out there that works. He/she will find "the one", the diet to deliver them into 'slimness nirvana'.

Top 10 Fad Diets

Dr Atkins Diet Revolution—Robert C. Atkins, MD

- Overview: low carb, high protein 1200-1800 calories. This calorie range would result in weight loss no matter what combination of foods.
- Pluses: It has simplicity. By eliminating carbs and sugar it takes care of big calorie foods.
- Minuses: Relies heavily on protein that puts body in ketosis. Headaches, bad breath, nausea and carb cravings. High in saturated fats, too low in fruits, whole grains, fibre and calcium.
- Long term success: high protein, low carb not maintained for life, there is a rebound if carbs reintroduced.

Mastering the zone—Barry Sears PhD

- Overview: insulin imbalances cause people to gain weight. If protein, carb and fat consumed in exact proportions 40/30/30, excess weight drops off. Average calories per day 1000-1700.
- Pluses: recommends lean protein sources and minimising saturated fat.
- Minuses: Carbs not forbidden but tiny portions, snack choices unappetising.
- Long term success: because the discipline and accuracy in getting exact ratios is very hard to sustain, long term success very challenging.

Eat right for your type—Peter D'Adamo ND

- Overview: theory of blood type differences requiring different nutrition. If wrong foods taken it's equivalent to a faulty blood transfusion. Recommended caloric intake varies widely day by day.
- Pluses: lean protein and several servings of fruit and vegetables.
- Minuses: experts say there is no evidence to support this theory and no link with blood type and disease.
- Long term success: hard-to-find foods and preparing for the family of different blood types challenging.

Sugar Busters! Cut Sugar to Trim Fat—H. Leighton Steward, C. Morrison et al

- Overview: Claims that carbs cause obesity and insulin resistance. The recommended caloric intake is only 1200 per day so that alone would result in weight loss.
- Pluses: Lean cuts of meat and fruit and vegetables recommended. Regular exercise too.
- Minuses: Carb rebound inevitable as with other high protein diets. Unrealistic restrictions proposed by diet.
- Long term success: because of the unsustainability of program, gain is likely.

Eat More, Weigh Less—Dean Ornish, MD

- Overview: High carb, very low in fat, primarily vegetarian. Premise that calories from fat make us fat. Calories from 1200 to 1350 per day.
- Pluses: Small percentage would be happy with this arrangement of low fat, high carb.
- Minuses: 55/20/25 split of carb/protein/fat is the mix of those most successful in losing and keeping off weight (according to National Weight Control Register), but this diet is too low in protein and fat.
- Long term success: Too low in dietary fat for this to be sustainable over the long term. Dietary fat needed for satiety and absorption of certain nutrients.

The Pritikin Weight Loss Breakthrough—Robert Pritikin (father Nathan deceased, originator of Pritikin's)

- Overview: very high volume of complex fibrous carbs, limiting fat intake to 10-15 percent of total calories.
- Pluses: lean cuts of meat which may limit heart disease, good fibre intake.
- Minuses: lots of fibre causes swelling of stomach quickly, which leads to fullness and less calories consumed. However satiety doesn't last. Weight maintenance is difficult because this regime can lead to overeating.
- Long term success: Not everyone can feel good on such a low fat diet, which makes the maintenance program quite hard.

The New Cabbage Soup Diet—Margaret Danbrot

- Overview: soup consisting of cabbage, onions, peppers, tomatoes, celery and one other specified food. Less than 1000 calories per day, only recommended for seven days.
- Pluses: apart from rapid weight loss, no other advantages.
- Minuses: weight loss temporary, nausea, light-headedness and gas, common side effects.
- Long term success: maintenance of weight loss near impossible. Lifestyle changes re healthy eating and exercise not discussed in plan.

The Grapefruit Diet—Originator unknown

- Overview: most popular word-of-mouth diet in the western world. Grapefruit believed to have miraculous fat-burning qualities, grapefruit at every meal. Only up to 800 calories per day, leading to dramatic weight loss.
- Pluses: grapefruit source of Vitamin C and high in fibre.
- Minuses: limits essential nutrients and not enough calories for good health.
- Long term success: Weight rebound is inevitable.

The New Beverley Hills Diet—Judy Mazel

- Overview: "food combining" or separating of certain foods are the key to this 1980's blockbuster. Putting the wrong foods together causes enzyme confusion. For first 35 days calories can vary widely per day.
- Pluses: only advantage is that weight loss assured as it is very low in calories.
- Minuses: extremely low in protein, vitamins and minerals and research does not support the digestive premise.
- Long term success: not sustainable as the caloric intake is too low and there's not a balanced choice of foods.

Neander-Thin: Eat like a caveman to achieve a lean, strong, healthy body—Ray Audette

- Overview: known as the "Caveman Diet" it claims that modern highly processed food causes obesity.
- Pluses: by eating whole foods one can gain in vitamins and minerals.
- Minuses: the theory linking carbs such as wheat and grain to obesity and other diseases is not supported in research.
- Long term success: carb cravings will eventually emerge when glycogen stores depleted. Weight gain likely.

Diet Devotee's Reading List

Here is a factitious set of titles to help you maintain a sense of humour through all of the diet disasters and other memorable highlights and lowlights of your adult life.
Note: do not ask your librarian for a reservation.

The No-torious Diet: NO Chocolate, NO Fried Food, NO Ice Cream, NO Pizza
by I.M Assadist

Fat will be in by the time I'm thin
by M.T. Glass Hollywood stars diet secret—starvation
by S. Velte & S.Kinanbones

Wishful Shrinking
by I. D. Reamdaily

The Haight Diet: Just Eat the Foods You Hate
by Professor Poopensheizer

I Don't have an eating problem: I Have a Problem NOT Eating: Autobiography of a Food Fetishist
by Ham Burger

The Fast Diet—If You are Fat Don't Eat—Fast!
by Guru Ima Breatharian

The De-stress diet

Breakfast
Half a grapefruit, 1 slice wholemeal toast, 60 oz skimmed milk.

Lunch
4 oz leaned broiled chicken, 1 cup steamed fish, 1 cup herb tea, 1 cookie.

Afternoon Snack
Rest of chocolate cookies, 2 huge scoops rocky road ice-cream topped off with hot fudge, nuts, cherries and whipped cream.

Dinner
Large cheese and pepperoni pizza with 2 servings of garlic bread, 3 milky way candy bars.

Bedtime Snack
The whole of the frozen strawberry cheesecake.

Diet Guidelines

1. If you eat a thing and no one sees you, it doesn't have any calories.
2. If you have a diet drink along with the Mars bar, then the calories from the candy bar are cancelled out by the drink.
3. If you eat with another person then the calories don't count if you don't eat any more than they do.
4. Food used for medicinal purposes are null and void of calories, hot toddies, candy lozenges and Sara Lee cheesecake (for stress).
5. By fattening up everyone around you, you look slimmer.
6. Movie-related snacks do not attach to you, they are part of the entertainment deal and belong to the movie experience.
7. Broken up cookies have no calories, they all escaped into the atmosphere in the process of being broken up.
8. If you're in the process of preparing food and you lick the bowl, the fork, the spatula or knife then they don't count as calories.
9. Foods that are frozen don't have calories because the calorie is a measure of heat. Examples are ice cream, cheesecake, lollypops and frozen pies.
10. Chocolate is a substitute food and can replace anything else.

Deconstructing Fad Diets

Some guidelines for resisting the seduction of the next fad diet

Diets weren't meant to be like holding down a second job

- **Don't** go for eating regimes that are as strict as the armed forces with a set of complicated rules to follow. Often you're successful at the beginning because you take the trouble to adhere to them. But you can't be that vigilant for too long and so after a few days or weeks, you'll begin to break those rules.
- **Don't** go for ones that restrict certain foods, tell you to eat in certain combinations, or to eat at certain times of the day.

If the calorie count is too low, pass

- **Don't** be wooed by a promise of losing 3 or more kilos in the first week. Too few calories means missing out on important nutrients which can impact on both your short and long-term health.
- **Don't** follow any plan that asks you to drop below 1500 calories a day unless you are under strict medical supervision.

Expensive supplements should not be critical

- **Do** go ahead and take a multi-vitamin a day for health insurance but anything more complex in the way of highly priced supplements claiming to ban block absorb reconstitute or zap! Fat for faster weight loss.
- Most weight loss supplements stretch the truth to its very edges and are no substitute for good balanced nutrition and enough exercise.

No effort means no effect

- **Do** remember that realistic long-term weight loss takes some serious application on your part. It effectively means a change in habits and lifestyle reducing intake of the high fat high calorie foods and exercising on a regular basis. Your weight loss will be slower but there's much more chance of keeping the weight off. This has to be a regime you can live with, not a 'fair weather' plan.
- **Do** run away if the plan is promising you effortless weight loss, the only weight you'll lose for good is the money from your wallet.

If it sounds crazy and too-good-to-be-true, then it probably is!

- **Don't** go near negative-calorie wonder foods or supplements, fat-dessicating pills, or diets that configure according to your eye colour, zodiac sign or shoe size.
- **Do** consider that these fads and scams are unfounded and quite ridiculous.

Scams

Synonyms for **Scam** (verb) victimise, swindle, rook, gyp, goldbrick, nobble, diddle, bunco, defraud, con.

Scam in other languages

French – escroquerie, escroquer (v)
Italian – Truffa, truffare (v)
German – schwindeln, masche (slang)
Portuguese – Fraude
Dutch – Zwendel, bedriegen
Spanish – timo, estafa, estafar (v)

What is a scam? It's a fraudulent business scheme or swindle. Fact: People lose large amounts of money every year by believing and investing in scams devised by scam artists. Scam artists are constantly applying their considerable talent for deception and guile to develop new scams and re-invent old scams. What's that they say "A fool and his money are soon parted" but in the early part of this millennium you don't have to be anyone's fool to be parted with large wads of your hard-earned money. Scams are like viruses. No matter how sophisticated our medical programs, those little old viruses always seem to stay ahead of the posse. Well that too can be said of the scam.

They were the snake oil-merchants of days gone by, who persuaded many that the stuff in the bottle could cure just about anything.

Scams prey on our vulnerabilities, our desire for wealth, status, improved attractiveness, health or safety. Sometimes it defies logic because what they are offering is not even something you want or need but the carrot they are dangling seems too good to pass up on.

Glossary of Scam terms

The following is a glossary of scamming terms:

Advance Fee Fraud,
"Send us your account details so we can transfer a disgustingly large amount of money into it"... after making a very convincing case for why a perfect stranger would want to do this for you in the first place. See 'Nigerian scam'.

Bait and Switch
Where the unwitting is offered an item or product which is not readily available then switched to a more expensive product. This is illegal under the trade practices act.

Blowing
See 'tele-fraud'.

Boiler Room
The HQ of the scam operation, which can resemble the frenetic quality of the share market.

Cold callers
Scammers who ring out of the blue and you're left wondering how they got your name.

Cramming
This is a form of credit card fraud where other charges are added to the cost of the product.

Dumping
See 'Modem Jacking'.

Dummy Bidding
Artificially raising the bidding price at auction by planting a dummy bidder. This is practised quite often at house auctions, in fact it was not uncommon for the vendor to act as the dummy bidder.

Escrow
This is a consumer protection scheme where any monies for an online auction are held by a third party until the goods are received and accepted.

False Billing
This is trading on us not being very vigilant and it doesn't only happen to individuals, businesses can be caught paying bogus invoices because they haven't bothered checking their validity.

Fax-Back Fraud
This is an unsolicited fax requesting the receiver return the fax to a 190 number. The transmission then takes an inordinate amount of time to be sent causing the cost to be far and over the normal cost of sending a fax e.g. charges by the minute as in STD.

Knock-off Product
Like a 'genuine' Rolex being offered as if it were the real thing at a slightly lower price than you would get the original. Now why would they be so nice? Because it's a fake!!

Modem Jacking
A consumer's modem is highjacked in the middle of trying to connect to the Net by another internet service provider (ISP) without their knowledge.

Mouse Trapping
This is where the computer code on the scammer's web page effectively locks up any functions you want to perform online and the only way out is to agree to go for the scammer's deal or else re-boot your computer.

Multi-Level Marketing
Not to be confused with pyramid selling this is a legitimate scheme where people make money by selling goods or services through a network of contacts. The reason it's different is because multi-level marketing is sales focused whereas pyramid schemes are based on the recruitment process and not the sales.

Nigerian Scam
See 'Advance Fee Fraud'.

Ponzi Scheme
See 'Pyramid scheme'.

Pump and Dump
See 'Ramping'.

Property Marketing
The real estate scams are usually marketed through get-rich-quick property seminars. A few telltale signs used as bait are 'no down payment' and 'no equity needed'.

Pyramid Scheme
The scammer makes his money in the recruitment process rather than flogging a real product or service.
It was Charles Ponzi who originally marketed this kind of scam in the 1920s see 'Ponzi Scheme'.

Ramping
This is where the unsuspecting consumer is provided with unsolicited information about stocks. The idea behind this is that the scammer can sell their own holdings for a profit when they've created their own run on the specified shares. It's like getting a tip on a horse race when the tipster looks like the jockey!

Shill
This is a person who poses as someone who's made money out of the scam, and sings its praises to the new prospective dupe. Like a testimonial it is a very powerful persuader.

Spam
Believed to have derived from Monty Python's Flying Circus where one of the characters gets annoyed from continually being offered Spam, a meat product in a tin. It's the unsolicited email messages that appear from nowhere. They are promoting 'penis enlargement', breast enhancement and often to the wrong gender. And many many other things under the sun.

Tele-Fraud
This covers any fraud which uses the phone as the medium. It's also known as BLOWING in reference to the phone slang word "the blower". See 'blowing'.

Telephone number scam
This is a scam involving either a 0055 or 190 number. Notification either arrives by post or online Congratulations you have won a holiday or some such please ring this number.
Calls to these numbers are well above the cost of normal STD numbers and of course you are given the usual run around being transferred or asked to wait and so on.

Two-Tier Marketing
This is the practice of selling real estate to the non-local for much above the local market price. It pays to be in the know. The two tiers refers to the actual value (tier one) and the promoted value (tier two).

Chain-Mail Malaise

I must add my thanks to whoever sent me the one about rats in the glue on envelopes cause I now have to get a wet towel with every envelope that needs sealing.

Also I scrub the top of every can I open for the same reason. I want to thank you who have taken the time and trouble to send me your chain letters over the past 12 months. Thank you for making me feel safe, secure, blessed and wealthy.

Because of your concern I no longer drink Moccha Moco because it can remove toilet stains.

I no longer drink Dipsi or Dr Dipper since the people who make these products are atheists who refuse to put "under God" on their cans.

I no longer use Heflon wrap in the microwave because it causes cancer.

I no longer check the coin return on pay phones because I could be pricked with a needle infected with AIDS.

I no longer use cancer-causing deodorants even though I smell like a water buffalo on a hot day.

I no longer go to shopping malls because someone will drug me with a perfume sample and rob me.

I no longer shop at Courget since they are French and don't support the Salvation Army.

I no longer answer the phone because someone will ask me to dial a number for which I will get a phone bill with calls to Jamaica, Uganda, Singapore, and Ukbekistan.

I no longer eat Finger-Lickin-Chickin because their chickens are actually horrible mutant freaks with no eyes or feathers.

I no longer have any sneakers, but that will change once I receive my free replacement pair from 'Like'.

I no longer buy expensive cookies from Leiman Varcus since I now have their recipe.

I no longer worry about my soul because I have 363,214 angels looking out for me and St Theresa's novena have granted my every wish.

Thanks to you, I have learned that God only answers my prayers if I forward an email to seven of my friends and make a wish within five minutes.

I no longer have any savings because I gave them to a sick girl who is about to die in the hospital (for the 1,387,258th time).

I no longer have any money at all, but that will change once I receive the $15,000 that Lycrasoft are sending me for participating in their special email program.

Yes I am so grateful to you that I will now return the favour.

Weight Loss Scams

The following weight loss advertising claims, when viewed in the harsh light of day, seem so wild and unsubstantiated, but obviously they play to our preparedness to believe in miracles and the old piece of wisdom.

"If I always do what I always did, I'll always get what I always got."

There's just no getting around it, not even at the height of self-delusion and the 'gullibility fill'. No miracle, no slimming nirvana: a place where you can eat, drink, make merry, never exercise and still have a perfect slim, toned body, no instant fix.

The only thing you'll be losing as you sleep if you fall for one of these diet scams is **Money**!!

Also there are real dangers to your health from some of these products. They can cause death and permanent damage to your internal systems. Even the herbal supplements must be treated with caution, if you want to see what products have been recalled search on www.dietfraud.com

Here are a few examples of the wild claims made by the diet scammers:

- Lose 54 pounds and 6 dress sizes in six weeks
- Lose weight as you sleep
- Eat all you want and still lose weight
- Lose off your hips and thighs, target your problem areas
- Scientific breakthrough, medical miracle
- Fat will just melt away!
- Miracle weight-loss patch
- Blocks Absorption of fat carbs calories
- Lose at least 3 kilos/10 pounds a week
- Gets rid of ugly cellulite
- Hard abs and no sweat
- Be slim forever

Spot the Diet Scam

Signs/Claims Reality	Check
Eat all your favourite foods–pizza, pasta, fried chicken, ice cream and still lose weight	NO. To lose weight you need to reduce the intake of high calorie foods.
No need to diet or exercise	NO. To lose weight you need to burn more calories than you take in so an adjustment in lowering food intake and upping exercise is de rigeur.
Guaranteed to work for everyone	NO. There's nothing that can make that promise.
Binds with food to block absorption of fat/carbs/sugar/calories	NO. As yet there's not a product on the market that can do that.
Lose unsightly fat permanently	NO. The only way to stay slim is to keep up a healthy eating and exercise program.
Target the cellulite/stubborn fat on hips/thighs/bottom	NO. Wearing a patch or applying cream will not do anything to target fatty deposits.
Lose up to 10 pounds/ 4 kilos a week	NO. Beware of any weight loss regime that promises anything more than between half a kilo to a kilo. Fast weight loss is not the way as it leads to even faster weight gain.

Supervision not required	NO. A for-real weight loss program would have this incorporated as part of the program. DIY-dieting is about as effective as the weekend handyman.
Words that are emotive "miraculous" "exclusive" "breakthrough"	NO. These are pressing your subliminal buttons to persuade you, BEWARE!
Wide ranging claims e.g. cure all	NO. By exaggerating wildly and claiming to be all things to all women, makes it all the more of a lie.
Testimonials from "Mrs Bloggs from Uluru" and "Dr Vorkin" with before and after shots	NO. There is no proof, even photos can be doctored; no evidence that this is a real physician and even experts in the field of weight loss are divided.
Send $$$$$$ now	NO. This is very unprofessional. You don't have any proof there is a product or that it works. Don't part with your money.
Sign up for XXXXX months	NO. Don't get into any long term contractual arrangements. It could prove costly if you want to get out of them.
Advertising outside the mainstream, mail order, magazine or online	NO. Because these are so ephemeral they can be scammed from some PO box in Beloxieville, or Nihil so once again beware.

"Whoever commits a fraud is guilty not only of the particular injury to him who he deceives, but of the diminution of that confidence which constitutes not only the ease but the existence of society."

Samuel Johnson

The Prostitution of Kindness

We live in a topsy-turvy, counterfeit world! Domestic violence, acts of violence against our nearest and dearest, is a greater statistical likelihood than acts of rage against those complete strangers who take advantage of us every single day.

Like a blue green algal bloom polluting all our waterways, niceness is the stock-in-trade of customer interfacing, be it the check-out-chick, the waiter, the receptionist, the used-car salesman and anyone else who has an interest in relieving us of either our money, or else persuading us to give them the support or backing thus conferring more power to them.

Insincerity is the currency in nearly all our social, economic and workplace dealings.

Smile! If you smile they won't mind parting with their money. Smile and you'll finagle them into this scheme or that. Look them in the eye and smile!

Charm them! Disarm them! They won't mind being ripped off so much if you do it with panache. After all, long after they have forgotten how you made them buy something completely useless they will still remember the way you made them feel liked, cherished, important.

Faking it! Fake orgasms, fraudulent schemes, synergistic connections, teamwork, and speed dating, fast food, instant service.

The smiling face of customer service delivery is linked to the business transaction, sorry to put it so bluntly. No matter how much one is led to believe that it's you, sweet loveable you who inspires all this niceness.

Just as the incredibly rich socialite is left wondering whether her suitors love her or her money, the customer/client should also carry a very big dose of scepticism about dollar-dazzling-smiles.

Take the frontline customer service person.

They spend their workday smiling and fawning over a procession of complete strangers; they feign friendship with co-workers whom they would not have crossed the road to greet in the natural order of things; and with their bosses and superiors they spend a considerable time biting down on retorts, holding back on what they would love to be able to say but give an appearance of cooperativeness and amiability.

"Have a nice day" to customers

"Of course that's not too much trouble" to colleague.

"Yes boss I'll drop everything and get on to it straight away" (even though you'd love to say something else.)

Alain de Botton, the English philosopher who has become somewhat of a celebrity and the author of "The Consolations of Philosophy" had this to say in a radio interview about "Status Anxiety".

"There's often a language of deceit in workplaces, like, 'Hey, everyone's having a great time here!' An acknowledgment that, actually, sometimes work is pretty horrible could make people happier than some saccharine picture that makes them worry, "What's wrong with me?"

What cost this saccharine insincerity and inanity? Chances are very high that this paragon of agreeableness drives home in a state of rage swearing and blinding at every traffic frustration, kicks the pet on the way through the door, shouts at the kids and picks an argument with the spouse.

'Being real' must out somewhere. Those less admired but much more real qualities, the letting down of the hair, the letting fly of invective, being able to tell that person be they the colleague, the boss or alternatively the client himself

"Where to get off." It's about setting limits and taking back one's personal power.

Take the bank manager or financial consultant who is all smiles and warmth when explaining how to invest one's funds in their particular establishment; the car salesman who can't seem to do enough for you when you're looking to buy a car; the insurance salesman who comes to your home and acts for all intents and purposes like a long-lost and much-loved relative; the Amway consultant, the man selling encyclopaedias or cable TV, the woman selling Tupperware or cosmetics, the politician door knocking at election time prepared to listen to your every concern all seemingly so interested and caring.

"I have this fantastic deal for you!
It will bring you lasting happiness! Invest in (substitute 'bank loan, used car, plastic paraphernalia, botox, insurance premium) and you will have what you really, really need and want."

Interestingly you will all have had experiences of being on the "money back guarantee", refund, claiming on insurance or appliance maintenance side of these business transactions. This however does not receive the same high levels of personal warmth or caring that epitomises the coal face of the "hard sell". In fact you may well get the proverbial run around, be left waiting on the phone, at the counter or be told "I have to get the manager" or "didn't you read the fine print? This is not covered" or "Sorry your warranty is out of date" or "It will take ninety days as we have to send it offshore."

"Your call is important to us (we've moved our call centre to Delhi)
An operator will be with you as soon as they are available."

"Sorry the terms of your insurance policy do not cover Acts of Dog."

But there are other indirect methods that indicate this pervasive "kindness of strangers to strangers", those that reach out to you in your living room, on your radio. Contrary to those of you who believe the world is just a nicer place all round, these people too have their own reasons for 'being nice', whether it be cash for

comment, or to help their ratings there is definitely a reason which has nothing to do with caring about YOU.
The radio opinion gurus, how very considerate of them to be so free with their opinions! My word, if I couldn't tune into this or that radio station I wouldn't know what to think about the affairs of the world!

"Thank you for listening.
Yes it's true that I have an opinion on everything and that sometimes I make comments for cash.
But I fulfil an important public service.
What would people think if I didn't tell them what to think?
There'd be anarchy and we can't have that."

The always-perky game show host (how do they keep up those levels of enthusiasm and dazzlement?) who appears to want to give money and prizes away, hand over fist to all the ordinary Joes and Joannas out there.

"Come on down! Have I got a deal for you today!"

Gurus of daytime deliverance, Dr Phil, Oprah, Ricky, those warm wonderful people who no matter how famous they are, come right into my living room, take the time to listen to all kinds of human dysfunctions and apply their considerable wisdoms and insights into problem solving and fixing what's broken. How kind, how compassionate!

"Why she looks me right in the eye when she says that!
She must be talking especially to me!"

The professional carers, the ones paid to listen, when they ask "How's your life been so far?" they want the long answer. The taxi meter is ticking over, so it's in their interest to nod and look you in the eye. The facilitator, the counsellor, the life coach, the psychoanalyst—all prepared to actively listen, to spend time each week allowing you to talk of your troubles, neuroses.

"I hear what you're saying. Tell me more. I'm here for you."

The New Age clairvoyant, crystal healer, tea leaves reader, tarot card decoder "They must really care about me, they are so intuitive about what I'm looking for".

"Ah my crystal ball
(substitute tea cup, tarot cards, astrological chart, rune stones, Ouija board) tells me that you will hear only what you want to hear so if I'm especially vague and watch your body language you will think I'm prophetic."

Online dating and personal columns promising romance and lasting love. Just a mouse click away to 'love ever after'. Yes, promise the ads and pop-ups, there is a soul mate out there for you, just waiting for you to make contact, let the grand romance begin!

"Your soul mate is waiting. Only a mouse click away. Has been waiting all his/her life for you to contact them. Do it now!
Let your love life begin and become blissfully happy."

Maybe I'm being rather brutal and it could well be that amongst the other snake-oil merchants there are genuine healers, dealers and warm-fuzzy feelers. But this book is an antidote to saccharine times, to marzipan layers of insincerity and fakery.

A letter received by the B&Q customer services department today.

Dear Sir/Madam

My congratulations to you on getting a yacht to leave the UK on 28th November 2004, sail 27,354 miles around the world and arrive back 72 days later.

Could you please let me know when the kitchen I ordered 96 days ago will be arriving from your warehouse 13 miles away?
Yours faithfully,

P Doff

The Three Biggest Lies

Three Biggest Check-Out-Chick Lies

- Tell me about your day, I really want to know.
- Serving customers all day is what gives my life meaning.
- I'm doing this job because I just love people (not because I need the money)

Three Biggest Marketing Lies:

- Immediate delivery? No problem.
- We treat every customer as if they were our most important.
- Customer service is what drives everything we do. (non profit?)

Three Biggest Advertising Lies:

- "Toxic sludge IS good for you." (trust us, would we mislead you?)
- You really need our product.
- If you use our product, you will have a movie star or model of your choice come to your door because they find you irresistible.

Three Biggest Daytime TV Guru Lies

- I'm doing this because I loooove people.
- I would listen to your 'twisted tales' even if I wasn't in front of an audience of millions.
- I do this for love, not money.

Three Biggest Insurance Salesman Lies

- I am here talking to you because I care.
- I am proposing you take this insurance out because it's essential to your peace of mind.
- Claiming on your insurance will be pain-free and done in days, no questions asked.

Three Biggest Phone Customer Service Lies

- "Your call is important to us."
- "Your call is important to us, you have been placed in a queue."
- "Your call is important to us, your call will be handled as soon as we have an available consultant."

Three Biggest Facilitator Lies

- Trust the process. Trust me.
- "I hear what you're saying." (yes but do you understand?)
- I'm doing this because I care.

Three Biggest Gameshow Host Lies

- I love being here every evening with a huge smile on my face.
- I want to give prizes away to Joe Nobodys because I'm a nice guy.
- I never ever get angry, upset or frustrated.

Three Biggest CEO Lies:

- I eat, live and breathe the company's vision and mission.
- I have absolutely no plans to trim the fat to pay for my job (by sacking staff).
- I single-handedly add value for the shareholder.

Three Biggest Large Company Lies:

- We place great importance on innovation and initiative.
- People are our greatest resource.
- We say 'let the marketplace decide'.

Three Biggest Small Company Lies:

- We have an entrepreneurial spirit here.
- The boss is just one of the workers, nothing special.
- Staying small is a conscious decision.

Three Biggest Politician's Lies:

- I will answer your questions with total honesty.
- I can state with absolute certainty that .... (fill in the blank)
- The government does not, and I say does not, waste the taxpayers' money.

Three Biggest Mail Order Lies:

- Delivery of your product will occur within 30 days of ordering.
- If you're not satisfied with our product we will guarantee a full refund.
- Of course we offer after sales service, guaranteed.

Three Biggest Retail Industry Lies:

- Our staff are courteous and considerate.
- We bend over backwards to help you with your problem.
- You will have no trouble getting a full refund for any returned goods (we don't insist you donate an organ or offer your firstborn).

Three Biggest Supermodel Lies:

- Women normally look like that.
- Women should look like that.
- Fasting and dieting is good for your health.

Three Biggest Beer Ads Lies:

- Drinking beer is for macho men only.
- You'll meet good lifelong friends drinking beer in a bar.
- Women think drunken loudmouths are sexy.

Your Call is Important to Us

"Dear We-Are-Best-of-Breed-Company,
I know my call is important to you, because you've now told me that every minute for the 48 minutes I've been on hold."

Hello, Welcome to the Psychiatric Hotline

If you are obsessive-compulsive, please press 1 repeatedly.

If you are co-dependent, please ask someone to press 2.

If you have multiple personalities, please press 3, 4, 5 and 6.

If you are paranoid-delusional, we know who you are and what you want. Just stay on the line so we can trace the call.

If you are schizophrenic, listen carefully and a little voice will tell you which number to press.

If you have a nervous disorder, please fidget with the # key until a representative comes on the line.

If you have amnesia, press 8 and state your name, address, phone number, date of birth, social security number and your mother's maiden name.

If you have post-traumatic stress disorder, slowly and carefully press 000.

If you have short-term memory loss, press 9. If you have short-term memory loss, press 9. If you have short-term memory loss, press 9. If you have short-term memory loss, press 9.

If you have a masochistic complex, please press "0" for the operator. There are 200 calls ahead of you.

If you are depressed, it doesn't matter which number you press. No one will answer.

Call Centres

Call centres have been dubbed the 'sweat shops of the 21st century'.

Mass production 'customer service', row upon row of workstations overseen and monitored by a supervisor who ensures they are meeting their quotas, a largely 'flexible' workforce i.e. casuals, is the human equivalent of the battery hen poultry industry.

When the ACTU (Australian Council of Trade Unions) set up a Call Centre Hotline (the Call centres have been largely non-unionised) to record complaints they included such things as:

- Unpaid training.
- Harassment and bullying.
- Petty time-keeping.
- Performance monitoring.
- Humiliation when unrealistic targets for sales and call times not met.
- Not being permitted to unionise.
- No tenure for long term casuals.

The way to avoid getting workers better conditions and tenure is to take the business offshore.

Moving call centres offshore is now common practice.

An excerpt from an article by Kirsty Needham a Consumer Reporter on July 13, 2005.

Delhi dialling makes tempers flare

The telephone ombudsman has been fielding gripes from consumers sick of dealing with Indian call centres.

"I don't want to talk to that person; they're in India," was the typical whinge, said the watchdog's quarterly newsletter...

The combination of thick regional accents and the absence of a customer service culture in India, were issues well-recognised by the industry, he said.

("Their English grammar is fantastic but the pronunciation is so different it is really hard even face-to-face, so on the telephone when they are sticking to procedures, it is a huge problem) he said."

Do you get unsolicited calls from someone representing Optus or another phone company in the night hours? Do they have a foreign accent?

Posting by KissorKill on CRACKER 8th March 2005

"I'm sick and bloody tired of having overseas call centres calling me and trying to shove Optus products and services (down my throat)."

Despite saying NO they just don't get it and have rung every day for past week. Why can't this Telco employ aussies to do the work instead of contracting the work to overseas call centres?"

"Telstra is set to confirm it will export another 500 Melbourne jobs to India."

The telecommunications giant did not return calls from Workers Online last Friday but industry sources insisted IBM GSA contracts had been terminated with the work going to Infosys and Aventail, both based in India."

Bugbears

Putting phone calls ahead of real customers
You patiently wait in line some place, you get to the front, you catch someone's attention, and then the phone behind the counter rings. All of a sudden, the phone call has become more important than you and it takes precedence over your issue.

The by-the-book treatment, or "I have to speak to the manager"
Company policies may be all very well as guidelines but when someone quotes you chapter-and-verse about why your request does not fall within the strict parameters of service or maintenance, it can lead to high levels of frustration for the customer. The real point about good customer service is surely to accommodate the diversity that exists in the human population. Employers who give their workers discretionary privileges, instead of having to go through the manager, are a recipe for 'good customer service'. For instance, Outback Steakhouse, making things work is the policy. If something is not to your liking at Outback, your waiter or waitress is empowered to fix it. They can give you a free drink, comp you a meal, etc. without having to go to their manager. Bending policy to make customers happy is the norm, not the exception, at this eatery.

The Phone-Tag-Run-Around
You ring your local retail store or hardware store to ask about a product in the home-delivered catalogue. You want to establish if they still have some in stock to save yourself a wasted trip. If the phone is answered, you are told to hold the line, then after some minutes, and you ask to be linked to the department of your choice, and you're told "Just transferring you now". You wait and wait and wait as the phone rings and rings and rings, or else you are treated to Muzak! Often it is a futile exercise which leaves you in serious doubt about how much this company is in the business of serving customers.

How's your day been so far?

Do you ever wonder if Rule #33 of Customer Service Manual for retail directs employees who interface with the customer to ask,

"How's your day been so far?"

Some even ask it when you are shopping at seven o'clock in the morning. "Sorry I don't have much to report—got up, went to the loo, threw on some trakkies and here I am".

Especially as these are supermarkets offering express lanes. Service with a "swift smile", the mass production line of processing the customer. Do you ever find it takes away from the seeming friendliness when as soon as your packages have been dealt with and the money has changed hands, you are immediately forgotten and the same words are being asked of the next customer in the queue with the same level of cheeriness,

"How's your day been so far?"

And you do feel rather constrained to keep the talk to a minimum. Why? well just because there are other customers breathing down your neck.

Do you ever feel tempted to take them at their word and instead of giving the standard automatic response,

"Fine"

You give a blow-by-blow of a "day from Hell"

"Well, I'm really glad you asked. People just seem to care about themselves these days so it's lovely to find someone who really cares, I've had a woeful day"

At which point you launch into your saga of woe giving yourself lots of time to go into the itty-bitty details. Having come to some kind of a finish to your tale and duly noting the customer service person's smile begin to fray at the edges, thank them profusely for caring, then as you go to leave, take note of whether they will greet the next customer with that same question,

"And how's your day been?"

Three Ducks

A guy walks into a bar holding three ducks. He sets them on the bar and orders a drink. After talking with the bartender for a while, the man excuses himself to use the restroom.

The bartender feels a tad awkward with just himself and three ducks at the bar, so he decides to make small talk with them.

He asks the first duck, "What's your name?"

"Huey," replies the duck.

"So, how's your day been?"

"Oh, I've had a great day," replies Huey. "I've been in and out of puddles all day."

The bartender asks the second duck, "What's your name?"

"Duey," replies the duck.

"So, how's your day been?"

"Oh, I've had a great day," replies Duey. "I've been in and out of puddles all day."

The witty bartender says to the third duck,

"So I guess your name is Louie?"

The duck replies, "No, I'm Puddles."

Telemarketers – How to get your own back

Allow them to go through their spiel all the way to the end with only the requisite uh-huh or "how fascinating" At last when they put the hard word on you for a sale, ask if they'll marry you. When that be-flusters them, tell them your mummy told you never to give out your credit card details to a stranger. If they insist on loaning you money, let them know you're a bankrupt and you could sure do with some lucre.

If they introduce themselves as Bill Backy from the Gazoo Company, ask them to spell their name. Do it slowly as if you're writing it down, then ask them to spell the company's name. Then ask where they are located, and ask them to spell the address. Keep this up until they leave you alone.

This is one that works better if you're male:
Telemarketer: Hi my name's Dana and I'm with Wiggle and Woggle services. Silence from you for a few heartbeats, "Okay" in a really husky voice "What are you wearing?" Telemarketer (Click!)

Sing out, in tones of abject pleasure and surprise "Dana! Is that you? Oh my lord! Dana how have you BEEN?" This will terrify Dana as her mind will be doing flip-flops trying to recall where she knows you from. (Click!)

Just say 'No' over and over but modulate the way you say it. Sometimes even when they're still in full flight. It's a lot of fun and you can keep doing it until they hang up.

If their opening line is, "How are you today?" reply "Why do you want to know?" Or if you have time you can tell them "I'm glad you asked because it's just shocking that people don't seem to care these days, and I have so many personal problems. Have you got half an hour?" If they try to steer you back to the 'sell' just persist with your own stuff.

If BCA insurance is trying to sign you up for a Family and Friends Plan, reply and make it as sinister as you can, "But I don't have any friends, could you be my friend?"

If it's a carpet cleaning franchise: "Can you get blood out? Can you get out goat's blood? What about human blood?" or alternatively "Sorry my floors are made of marble".

Answer the phone. As soon as they begin with the palaver, put the receiver down then scream "Oh my god!" then hang up.

Tell the telemarketer you can't talk to them right now, you're busy but could you have their number and you'll call them back. When they explain that they are not at liberty to give out the number, you say "I suppose you can't have anyone interrupting you when you're at work" and the person will agree. You say "Now you know how I feel" and hang up.

Say "Speak up!" and just keep saying it until they're screaming into the phone then hang up.

Tell them you work for a consumer affairs office and you are taping all calls.

"Can't come to the phone right now"

These suggested messages are a way of taking back the power. If that telemarketer can ring you at home, make sure you are armed and ready with a "killer" response.

Hi. This is John: If you are the phone company, I already sent the money. If you are my parents, please send money. If you are my financial aid institution, you didn't lend me enough money. If you are my friends, you owe me money. If you are a female, don't worry, I have plenty of money.

Hi. John's answering machine is broken. This is his refrigerator. Please speak very slowly and I'll stick your message to myself with one of these magnets.

Hello. You are talking to a machine. I am capable of receiving messages. My owners do not need siding, windows, or a hot tub, and their carpets are clean. They give to charity through the office and don't need their picture taken. If you're still with me, leave your name and number and they will get back to you.

This is not an answering machine—this is a telepathic thought recording device. After the tone, think about your name, your reason for calling and a number where I can reach you, and I'll think about returning your call.

"Hi, this is George. I'm sorry I can't answer the phone right now. Leave a message, and then wait by your phone until I call you back."

This is the Metropolitan Opera Amateur Audition Hotline. After the tone, sing 'Vesti la Giubba' and 'La Donna e Mobile.'

We're sorry. You have reached an imaginary number. Please rotate your phone 90 degrees and try again.

Joe here. I'm home right now, I'm just screening my calls. So start talking and if you're someone I want to speak with I'll pick up the phone. Otherwise, well, what can I say?

Hi, it's a great day and I'm out enjoying it right now. I hope you are too. The thought for the day is 'Share the love.' Beep.

Uh, yeah... this is the VD clinic calling.... Speaking of being positive, your test is back. Stop sharing the love.

I can't come to the phone now because I have amnesia and I feel stupid talking to people I don't remember. I'd appreciate it if you could help me out by leaving my name and telling me something about myself. Thanks.

I can't come to the phone right now because I'm down in the basement printing up a fresh new batch of twenty dollar bills. If you need any money, or if you just want to check out my handiwork, please leave your name, number, and how much cash you need after the tone. If you're from the Department of the Treasury, please ignore this message.

Thank you for calling 555-2322. If you wish to speak to Tim, push 1 on your touch-tone phone now. If you wish to speak to Lynn, push 2 on your touch-tone phone now. If you have a wrong number, push 3 on your touch-tone phone now. All of this button pushing doesn't do anything, but it is a good way to work off anger, and it makes us feel like we have a big-time phone system.

Dr Phil's Inner Peace

Dr. Phil proclaimed the way to achieve inner peace is to finish all the things you have started. So I looked around my house to see things I started and hadn't finished and before leaving the house this morning I finished off a bottle of Merlot, a bottle of White Port, a bottle of Baileys, a bottle of Kahlua, a package of Tim Tams, the remainder of both Prozac and Valium prescriptions, the rest of the Cheesecake, some Sao's and a box of Chocolates.

You have no idea how freaking good I feel.

Customer Service – going the extra mile

A man was in a long line at the grocery store, and as he got to the register he realised he had forgotten to get condoms, so he asked the checkout girl if she could have some brought up to the register.

She asked, "What size condoms?" The customer replied that he didn't know.

She asked him to drop his pants. He did, she reached over the counter, grabbed hold of him and called over the intercom, "One box of large condoms, Register 5."

The next man in line thought this was interesting, and like most of us, was up for a cheap thrill. When he got to the register, he told the checker that he too had forgotten to get condoms, and asked if she could have some brought to the register for him. She asked him what size, and he stated that he didn't know.

She asked him to drop his pants. He did, she gave him a quick feel, picked up the intercom and said, "One box of medium-sized condoms, Register 5."

A few customers back was this teenage boy. He thought what he had seen was way too cool. He had never had any type of sexual contact with a live female so he thought this was his chance. When he got to the register he told the checker he needed some condoms. She asked him what size and he said he didn't know.

She asked him to drop his pants and he did. She reached over the counter, gave him one quick squeeze, then picked up the intercom and said

"Cleanup, Register 5!"

Barber Shop

A guy sticks his head into a barbershop and asks, "How long before I can get a haircut?" The barber looks around the shop and says, "About 2 hours." The guy leaves.

A few days later the same guy sticks his head in the door and asks, "How long before I can get a haircut?" The barber looks around at the shop full of customers and says, "About 3 hours." The guy leaves.

A week later the same guy sticks his head in the shop and asks, "How long before I can get a haircut?" The barber looks around the shop and says, "About an hour and a half." The guy leaves.

The barber who is intrigued by this time, looks over at a friend in the shop and says, "Hey, Bill. Follow that guy and see where he goes."

A little while later, Bill comes back into the shop, laughing hysterically.

The barber asks, "Bill, where did he go when he left here?"

Bill looks up, tears in his eyes and says, "Your house!"

Customer Service Fatigue

There are of course two sides to the prostitution of kindness, to the inanity of the person delivering the service having to do it with a "smile" and a great deal of forbearance at times.

After decades of indoctrinating the service worker into the creed of "the customer is always right", there is an understandable backlash from those who are perfectly poised to know how clueless the customer can be.

Surely, it is a given that working in any industry day-in-day-out gives the probability of more expertise in that field than the consumer.

The following are antidotes for those who are suffering from Customer Service Fatigue and would relish the opportunity to say exactly what they're thinking.

The Customer is hardly ever right

Customer: "I've been ringing 0700 2300 for two days and can't get through to enquiries, can you help?"

Operator: "Where did you get that number from, sir?"

Customer: "It was on the door to the Travel Centre."

Operator: "Sir, they are our opening hours."

Samsung Electronics Caller: "Can you give me the telephone number for Jack?"

Operator: "I'm sorry, sir, I don't understand who you are talking about."

Caller: "On page 1, section 5 of the user guide, it clearly states that I need to unplug the fax machine from the AC wall socket and telephone Jack before cleaning. Now, can you give me the number for Jack?"

Operator: "I think you mean the telephone point on the wall."

RAC Motoring Services Caller: "Does your European Breakdown Policy cover me when I am travelling in Australia?"

Operator: "Doesn't the product give you a clue?"

Caller (enquiring about legal requirements while travelling in France): If I register my car in France, do I have to change the steering wheel to the other side of the car?"

Directory Enquiries Caller: "I'd like the number of the Argoed Fish Bar in Cardiff please."

Operator: "I'm sorry, there's no listing. Is the spelling correct?"

Caller: "Well, it used to be called the Bargoed Fish Bar but the 'B' fell off."

Then there was the caller who asked for a knitwear company in Woven.

Operator: "Woven? Are you sure?"

Caller: "Yes. That's what it says on the label: Woven in Scotland."

On another occasion, a man making heavy breathing sounds from a phone box told a worried operator: "I haven't got a pen, so I'm steaming up the window to write the number on."

Caller: "I deleted a file from my PC last week and I have just realised that I need it. If I turn my system clock back two weeks will I have my file back again?"

There's always one. This has got to be one of the funniest things in a long time. I think this guy should have been promoted, not fired. This is a true story from the WordPerfect Helpline, which was transcribed from a recording monitoring the customer care department. Needless to say the Help Desk employee was fired. However, he/she is currently suing the WordPerfect organisation for "Termination without Cause". Actual dialogue of a former WordPerfect Customer Support employee. (Now I know why they record these conversations!):

Operator:	"Ridge Hall, computer assistance; may I help you?"
Caller:	"Yes, well, I'm having trouble with WordPerfect."
Operator:	"What sort of trouble?"
Caller:	"Well, I was just typing along, and all of a sudden the words went away."
Operator:	"Went away?"
Caller:	"They disappeared."
Operator:	"Hmm. So what does your screen look like now?"
Caller:	"Nothing."
Operator:	"Nothing?"
Caller:	"It's blank; it won't accept anything when I type."
Operator:	"Are you still in WordPerfect, or did you get out?"
Caller:	"How do I tell?"
Operator:	"Can you see the C: prompt on the screen?"
Caller:	"What's a sea-prompt?"
Operator:	"Never mind, can you move your cursor around the screen?"
Caller:	"There isn't any cursor: I told you, it won't accept anything I type."
Operator:	"Does your monitor have a power indicator?"
Caller:	"What's a monitor?"
Operator:	"It's the thing with the screen on it that looks like a TV. Does it have a little light that tells you when it's on?"
Caller:	"I don't know."
Operator:	"Well, then look on the back of the monitor and find where the power cord goes into it. Can you see that?"
Caller:	"Yes, I think so."
Operator:	"Great. Follow the cord to the plug, and tell me if it's plugged into the wall."
Caller:	"Yes, it is."
Operator:	"When you were behind the monitor, did you notice that there were two cables plugged into the back of it, not just one?"

Caller: "No."

Operator: "Well, there are. I need you to look back there again and find the other cable."

Caller: "Okay, here it is."

Operator: "Follow it for me, and tell me if it's plugged securely into the back of your computer."

Caller: "I can't reach."

Operator: "Uh huh. Well, can you see if it is?"

Caller: "No."

Operator: "Even if you maybe put your knee on something and lean way over?"

Caller: "Oh, it's not because I don't have the right angle, it's because it's dark."

Operator: "Dark?"

Caller: "Yes, the office light is off, and the only light I have is coming in from the window."

Operator: "Well, turn on the office light then."

Caller: "I can't."

Operator: "No? Why not?"

Caller: "Because there's a power failure."

Operator: "A power, a power failure? Aha, Okay, we've got it licked now. Do you still have the boxes and manuals and packing stuff your computer came in?"

Caller: "Well, yes, I keep them in the closet."

Operator: "Good. Go get them, and unplug your system and pack it up just like it was when you got it. Then take it back to the store you bought it from."

Caller: "Really? Is it that bad?"

Operator: "Yes, I'm afraid it is."

Caller: "Well, all right then, I suppose. What do I tell them?"

Operator: "Tell them you're too stupid to own a computer."

Things you wanted to say to the customer but left unsaid

Customer service employees put up with a great deal from Joe Customer. When the customer/client/consumer comes into their store and treats them like s**t, there's a good deal that goes through their minds, but can't be said for fear of losing their jobs, here's a sample.

You are obviously smarter than me, so if YOU can't figure it out, what the hell makes you think I can?

No, sir, I'm not hard-of-hearing, neither am I stupid. You just don't speak good English.

Do you notice that your bad behaviour is embarrassing your wife?

Do you want me to go ahead and call the manager, or do you want me to wait till you're REALLY pissed off?

I can tell you right now I'm not going to give you very good service, because I think you're drunk or possibly on drugs, and frankly, you scare the hell out of me.

No, sir, I can't do maths in my head, but I can spell diarrhoea.

I realize I'm ignoring you, but you're in here every three days with your spoilt kid and you never buy anything you don't return.

Shame on you for using such language in front of your children.

You've been waiting 30 minutes? Why didn't you use the time to find it yourself?

If I were as smart as you THINK I should be, I'd be making a lot more money than I am now.

Don't complain about the f**king line up and then fumble through your purse for 5 minutes when you finally have your order taken.

No, really, I want you to call me every day to ask what time we close when we are open 24 hours a day.

Oh yes, please let me search out that item that we haven't had for eight years and then bitch to me for a half hour about how we had it yesterday. We didn't, arsehole!

Should I hand you the fries or shove them up your fat arse?

Well now that you've ordered your large popcorn with extra butter and 2 large chocolate bars, I'm sure that the large DIET coke will really do you some good and cancel out the 10,000 calories you are about to eat while you sit on your ass and do sweet f**k all nothing for the next two hours.

You know I am off work and yet you insist on motioning to me... Well for some reason I have gone blind and can't see you.

Maybe you should buy a full length mirror before buying all that junk food.

No you moron, I don't work here! I'm only here because I like to wear this name tag, sweep floors and hang around 10 to 12 hours a day for the fun of it!

The food will never look like it does in the pictures. The food in the picture was plastic.

Types of people who call for IT support

From someone in the IT Helpdesk business who spent years analysing the kinds of persons who ring the Helpdesk. His scientific findings:

1. "The Expert": Userus expertia

"The Expert" user is the curse of most IT support establishments. Experts try out something they heard about from "the bloke in the pub," an unqualified expert on everything who offers advice to anyone who will listen. Experts usually make a complete mess of their systems when they follow the bloke's advice. Then they compound the problem by trying to fix it themselves, often destroying their machines. As a last resort, they call the help desk and demand that their machines be replaced or mended immediately, as they have urgent work that can't wait. There has been an Expert at every place I have worked. I leave it to you to decide who your resident Expert is.

2. "The Fiddler": Userus manipulata

The motto of "The Fiddler" is: "I wonder what happens if...." I've placed these callers next because they are the most closely related to the Expert. These callers don't realize that some files actually make their computers work. If they don't recognize a file as one of their own, they delete it and are surprised when something then stops working. Unlike the Expert, they don't say anything about the problem; you only discover it months later from a casual remark, such as, "Oh no, that hasn't worked for ages. I meant to call you." Fiddlers are usually very pleasant people who will drive you mad.

3. "The Mouse": Userus rodentia

"The Mouse" is more common than the previous two and fortunately less harmful. For this species of caller, the big grey box is a source of blind terror. I can remember talking on the phone to a Mouse at a UK communications company. She had worked in a telephone exchange for years and was suddenly given a PC to help her. She had not asked for it and didn't want it. The screen was making strange noises, and she was concerned. "I don't want it to explode or anything," she wailed. "No," I said patronisingly, "they don't explode. There's no explosive in them." Then I heard a loud "Bang!" through the phone. "What was that?" I asked. "My screen has just exploded," she replied.

4. "The Train Spotter": Userus geekissimus

"The Train Spotter" is most often the offspring of an Expert and a Fiddler. These callers are usually harmless and don't have many computer problems. What they do have is an IT magazine, which they have read from cover to cover. The Train Spotter will invariably corner an unsuspecting help desk tech and proceed to bore the tech rigid by sharing their knowledge. The main difference between Train Spotters and other callers is that Train Spotters do not usually phone the help desk, they visit in person. I'm not quite sure what they want from the help desk, but they take up a lot of time asking various questions about new innovations, about which I usually know nothing. I have found no explanation for the existence of this user other than that the Expert and Fiddler conceived the Train Spotter on a trip to a computer trade fair.

5. "The Paranoid User": Userus newbigata

"Paranoid Users" are convinced that the computer has an intelligence of its own and is out to get them. The machine is constantly doing something that causes a problem. The computer will maliciously alter their documents, obliterate all references to their passwords, and lose work they have saved. If a machine is ever going to break down, it will be while being used by a Paranoid. This species' one saving grace is determination. They never give up, as much as you wish they would.

6. "The I'm-building-a-case User": Userus fabricatum

"The I'm-Building-A-Case User" is grinding an axe to get some new gadget brought in to his department or have an old one taken away. They report hundreds of trivial problems, hoping upper management will buy them the latest all-singing and all-dancing machine. The real problem with this species of caller is the fact that they are usually not trying to replace computer equipment. This user doesn't see the difference between computers and any other piece of office equipment. I have often been required to pass opinions on all kinds of electrical equipment even after pointing out my lack of knowledge on the subject. I do not evaluate coffee makers. I do not drink coffee, and I know nothing about the black arts involved in its production.

7. "The Just-testing User": Userus gustulata

"The Just-Testing User" is not even using a computer but wants to test your knowledge and, if possible, trip you up. The best technique for dealing with this species is by answering questions with "I don't know." They cannot deal with this straight capitulation. Most Just-Testing users would love the chance to show your boss how useless you are or how little you know. They are thrilled when you give a wrong answer and will crow about it incessantly.

8. "Pig Pen": Userus perfumia

Based on the Charles M. Schulz Peanuts character, "Pig Pen" has the messiest, most unhygienic work area in the company. Pig Pen's personal hygiene is fine; it is only the workspace that is a hazard.

It is a graveyard for old coffee cups, half-eaten green sandwiches, used Kleenex, and mouldy sock collections. Pig Pens are some of the nicest and most technically able people you know. They usually give the help desk very little trouble except when their keyboard needs replacing, which is often. Pig Pen is a mainstay of most companies, the backbone of whatever department he or she works for. If that were not the case, the company would have let them go years ago.

9. "The I-don't-want-to-hear-that! User": Userus headinsandia

This is a rather curious species. They call, ask a question, and if they don't hear what they want, they take it personally. I always wonder why they ask, if they don't want to know the answer. It does not seem to matter that what they want is not possible. All they want is to hear the answer they're looking for.

10. "The End-of-my-tether User": Userus adlimitus

This is the angriest but, perversely, often the easiest to deal with. After spending weeks attempting to resolve their own queries, they finally swallow their pride and call the help desk. Calls from this type of user usually end in one of three ways:

1. The problem's solution can be found simply by reading page 1 of his instruction manual, which, of course, the caller has not done.

2. The caller is informed that the operation she is trying to perform cannot be performed with the equipment or software that she has.

3. The caller has already found a solution but phoned the help desk to let you know how frustrated, mad, or unsatisfied he is.

Feel Good Blues

"How are you today?"
"What can I get you?"
Fatuous vacant smiles from
check-out-chicks and air hostesses
"Will you have fries with that?"
squawks the disembodied box
at the Fast-Food-Drive-Thru.

Advertising hype!!
Snap frozen, Processed Tripe!!
Save Save Save
Twenty-four months interest free
Two for the price of one
99.9% Fat free
100% Natural
Absolutely no preservatives
Free Range!
Exotic!
Ma-Crobiotic!

Buzz words coming at you like
staccato machine gun fire
Rat-a-tat-tat
Self-Empowerment
Achieve and Succeed
Value Add.

Unguents, ointments and treatments
Rejuvenating,
rehydrating,
replenishing
You can just feel it doing you good.
Promise of a wrinkle-free eternity,
Yes you're still gonna die
but you're gonna be
a good looking
Corpse!

Video hits, MTV
Nubile swaying bodies
The latest rap and pop and reggae
There's a party in your living room
'Come join in' they croon
Rock your body,
Feel that beat!

Self-help Gurus
Talking heads
Ricky, Oprah and Dr Phil
Showing you how
To shape up,
slim down,
kick the habit,
Buck Up
Daytime deliverance
from all Your woes.
"Go girl!"

Voice recording over the phone
Telling you
With pleasing sincerity
"We value your call,
You are important to us"
Muzak, muzak, muzak
"Your call is important to us, still."

Glossy magazines
Brad and Angelina
J Lo and Ben
David and Posh
All dressed to the nines
but
Something ain't right in
Paradise.

Yeah Baby
Everywhere you look
Every place you go
Hear it on the telly and the radio
Smarmy Smiling Simpering
They want you bad, yeah
They want you bad.

Hallellulia! Hallelulia!
Then
Why do I still feel like
S**T?

What it Really Means

'Then you should say what you mean,' the March Hare went on. 'I do,' Alice hastily replied; 'at least, at least I mean what I say, that's the same thing, you know.' 'Not the same thing a bit!' said the Hatter. 'Why, you might just as well say that "I see what I eat" is the same thing as "I eat what I see!"'

Alice's Adventures in Wonderland, 1865

"Euphemism is a euphemism for lying."

Bobbie Gentry

Between euphemisms, doublespeak, jargon, mumbo jumbo, business buzzwords, bureaucratese and the "credibility gaps and gullibility fills" between men and women, there is definitely a need for a chapter on decoding, decrypting, translating the terms and phrases.

Here is an alphabetical listing of the many ways words can deceive, equivocate, defraud, dissemble, dissimulate:

Ambiguity,
Headline "Prostitutes appeal to Pope".

Acronyms, DWY
= "Driving while yakking" on cell phone, nearly as dangerous as DUI; or GMO "genetically modified organism".

Bureaucratese
"The clerk opened the letter with a knife " in bureaucratese this would be "The civil servant was empowered to facilitate the opening of written correspondence with a sharp utensil".

Buzzwords
"Paradigm shift" meaning the latest greatest management theory that has taken over and all must rush to follow.

Clichés
"At the end of the day" voted the most irritating cliché in 2004.

Contradictions
"He who hesitates is lost" vs "look before you leap".

Doublespeak
"Collateral damage" meaning civilian casualties.

Euphemism
"Renovator's delight" in real estate means a dump.

Fallacy
1. Some acts of killing human beings are legal in this state.
2. Some acts of killing human beings are illegal in this state.
3. Therefore some acts of killing human beings are both legal and illegal in this state.

Gobbledygook, "we have retrocessed, reponed and restored Executors and Assignees" – Bank of Scotland.

Hyperbole
"Extravagant exaggeration" is itself a form of hyperbole.

Inanity
"Let me say, for the record and without a word of equivocation that..."

Jargon
"Billable hours" is the lawyer's way of charging the client which bears no correlation to the real amount of time spent on the case.

Longwindedness
"The project is structured around a multifaceted incremental work plan combining novel content design based on new pedagogical paradigms."

Mumbo Jumbo
In a speech to a startled audience at the 150th anniversary dinner of the British Medical Association in 1982, Prince Charles declared that a good doctor 'must have the feel and touch which makes it possible for him to be in sympathetic communication with the patient's spirits'.

Presumption
- Women earn less than men earn for doing the same work.
- Oprah Winfrey is a woman.
- Therefore, Oprah Winfrey earns less than male talk-show hosts.

Quoting Sources
It's not the quoting of sources itself that is inherently deceptive, it's the kind of source that sets up a bias in reporting or quotes an expert who can support one's product or line of reasoning.

Rhetoric
Because of its open-ended appeal to reason, emotion or character, rhetoric is a powerful tool. In the wrong hands it is positively dangerous. "With us, life is stable and predictable. Without us, we will reap the whirlwind. Without us, radical fundamentalists will take our place."

Sophistry
A subtly deceptive reasoning or argumentation. There is inclined to be rather a lot of this kind of thing in the New Age movement.

Tautology
"If neither Jack Spratt or his wife, Pat, came to the party, then Jack Spratt didn't come to the party.

Untruth
It's a falsehood, a lie, a departure from the truth. It's no longer a question of if we lie, but whether we can detect the truth of a thing any more.

Vagueness
Paradox of the balding head. At what point of losing one's hair do you describe the man as bald?

Weasel words
Words that suck the meaning out of the words they are linked with "virtually everyone" "nearly everybody".

Yimmer Yammer
"Isn't it about time to end all of the Pointless Yimmer Yammer, Back-Stabbing, Name-Calling Drivel?"

Tips for good writing

Comparisons are as bad as clichés.
Don't be redundant; don't use more words than necessary; it's highly superfluous.
Be more or less specific.
Understatement is always best.
One-word sentences? Eliminate.
Analogies in writing are like feathers on a snake.
The passive voice is to be avoided.
Go around the barn at high noon to avoid colloquialisms.
Even if a mixed metaphor sings, it should be derailed.
Who needs rhetorical questions?
Exaggeration is a billion times worse than understatement.

Legalese to layman-ease

A young boy walked up to his father and asked,
"Dad? Does a lawyer ever tell the truth?"

The father thought for a moment.
"Yes, son," he replied,
"Sometimes a lawyer will do anything to win a case."

The lawyer's jargon and what it means for you if you ever have the #$%^ fortune to need their services:

Ad infinitum,
A Latin term meaning 'forever', which is how long your lawyer intends to keep your case going.

Affidavit
It's a written and notarised statement and whether true or a pack of lies, is taken 'as if it were true' because you swore it was in front of a notary.

Arbitration
This is another way of resolving disputes.
Both parties agree to abide by the arbitrator's decision, he is generally an ex-judge whose best days are over.

Bench
Hardly what it suggests. No this is the comfortable seat the judge gets to luxuriate in as he lords it over the court.

Beyond a reasonable doubt
This is the tug-of-war the lawyers on both sides of a trial are involved in, attempting to prove the other side is lying more than they are.

Bill-able hours
The number of hours billed to the client that is not to be confused with the time actually spent working on the case. The lawyer uses a complex formula to arrive at the billable hours. Hours actually working on case + time spent thinking about case whilst lunching + lawyer's car expenses X 4.

Capital punishment
A euphemism for 'cut off his head! gas him, hang him, take his life!' which is handed down by the judge, the state. In many countries it is outlawed however in the US it's alive and well, especially in Texas.

Caveat rumpus
A Latin term for 'watch your arse!' Something that becomes second nature in the legal profession.

Community property
Describes the property acquired by a couple during their marriage that is then appropriated by the lawyers during their divorce.

Complaint
This humble C word covers a multitude.
It describes what the lawyer first files on behalf of his client in order to get his day in court, but it also describes the constant dissatisfactions the client has about his defence.

Confession
What the accused finally decides to admit to when worn down by the endless pratings and legalese of the lawyers and can't stand another moment of the brain numbing process. "I did it! I did it! Take me away quick!"

Conflict of interest
A very serious matter. If one lawyer discovers that the person sitting on the other side of the court is paying his lawyer far more than what he's getting.

Contempt of court
A strange one. It's as if the court is a person you must be respectful of, otherwise the judge will charge you with contempt. Depending on what kind of a wig-day the judge is having he can hand out a slap on the wrist or hard labour to the contemptee. And watch out, if you object, his gavel will come down and he'll double or treble the penalty!

Cross examination
An opportunity for the lawyer to do his sadistic best to discomboobilate the witness of the moment, using every piece of skulduggery in the book, like a gorilla playing with a kitten!

Culpa lata
Another Latin term meaning 'gross negligence'. The lawyer who leaves his client with a little cash remaining is said by his colleagues to be 'culpa lata' setting up a dangerous precedent in law.

Defendant
For criminal cases, the person accused of committing said crime/s. In civil law, it's the poor misfortunate getting served with a lawsuit.

Directed verdict
The judge intercedes and directs the jury to come back with a certain verdict. Why? Because he considers that one or the other or both lawyers did not do a good job in representing the parties at hand.

Divorce
A tricky time in a couple's married life. On top of a lot of negative emotions, pile a couple of bad lawyers looking to make a buck out of the ill-feeling.

Duces tecum
A Latin term meaning 'bring with you'. Most commonly used in the initial meeting with the lawyer when you 'duces tecum your cheque book'.

Due process
The rather precious but unrealistic notion that laws and all surrounding matters be fair to all parties concerned.

Embezzle
If a citizen embezzles and gets caught with his hand in the till, then that is a crime. If the lawyer fleeces his client/s that is perfectly legal.

Ex parte communication
"Don't get caught bribing the judge or juror" in Latin.

Expert witness
An expert at tailoring his testimony to exactly suit the requirements of the lawyer picking up his tab.

Felony
The punishment for this is in having to get a lawyer to represent you.

Garnishment
Seizing a person's salary or property in order to pay off his or her outstanding balance to the lawyer.

Gavel
That impressive wooden hammer which the judge loves to brandish when he's bringing the court to order or driving home a point. A gavel-less judge wouldn't be nearly as authoritative!

Grounds for divorce
Discovery by one spouse that the other is having an affair with a lawyer.

Harassment
One person's harassment is another's vicarious pleasure. Unwelcome advances for one person are the much-appreciated advances for another. So needless to say, it's a subjective matter.

Hearsay evidence
Third party 'what someone heard about someone or something but neither saw nor heard first-hand' not admissible in court.

Indefensible
The primary behavioural trait commonly found in all lawyers.

Insolvent
Impoverished, broke, ruined, destitute, and busted, out of money. The financial condition of the client after the lawsuit is finally over.

Intestate
Dying without a will, thereby leaving your inheritance to the lawyers.

Joint custody
Upon being retained to represent the client, the lawyer is said to have obtained joint custody of client's bank account.

Jurisprudence
The science of converting the client's money into the lawyer's money.

Jury
A group of six or twelve everyday citizens, who couldn't figure out how to finagle their way out of jury duty, must now try and figure out which lawyer is lying the least.

Lawyer
"A lawyer is a liar with a permit to practice." Anonymous

Leading question
A question posed by a lawyer that suggests an answer. Such as asking the client "will you be paying by cash or by check?"

Mediation
An alternative method for resolving disputes between parties in which a neutral third party called the mediator attempts to facilitate a settlement. When the parties fail to reach an agreement, they are free to hammer each other with a lawsuit.

Mitigating circumstances
When the lawyer finds out you've run out of money and drops your case like a hot potato.

Negligence
Legal principle that holds that everyone, with the notable exception of lawyers and judges who are exempt from same, have a duty to ensure that their actions do not cause harm to others.

Negotiations
The act of determining whether the lawyer will take 50% or 60% of the money awarded to his or her clients.

Next of kin
A person you can borrow money from to help pay your lawyer bills.

Parole
The supervised release of prisoners before their terms are over, ensuring that lawyers will have a steady supply of repeat customers.

Penalty phase of the trial
The part of the trial when the lawyers start talking.

Perjury
When a lawyer's client actually gets caught lying under oath.

Plaintiff
The person who initiates a lawsuit. Known as the "suer."

Prima facie
Latin for "at first sight," as in when you first knew you were screwed when you met your public defender for the first time.

Probate
The formal certificate given by the probate court that attests that the will has been validated and that the lawyers can now divvy up the estate between them.

Pro bono
Work done for compassionate reasons without a fee to the client. A rare enough event and more likely to be the preserve of a large law firm.

Pro se
Latin phrase that means "for himself." It has been said that a person who represents himself in court is said to have a fool for a lawyer. But who's really going to notice the difference anyway?

Prostitute
A person who screws another person for money. See "Lawyer".

Punitive damages
Money awarded to a victim intended to punish a defendant and stop that business or individual from repeating the same kind of disgraceful conduct that lawyers get away with every single day.

Quid pro quo
Latin for "something for something." Generally an agreement between the lawyer and the judge wherein the lawyer slides the judge some cash under the table in exchange for letting the lawyer's client off the hook; or an agreement between lawyer and client wherein client slides lawyer money to slide to the judge to get the client out of hot water.

Res Ipsa Loquiter
Latin for "the thing speaks for itself".

Sequester
The act of locking a group of jurors in a room and then expecting them to all agree on a verdict after they have been subjected to countless hours of confusing testimony, conflicting statements and legal mumbo jumbo they don't understand and couldn't care less about.

Slander
Calling a lawyer a cheat and a crook when the correct verbiage would have been a shyster and a scoundrel.

Supersedeas
Latin for when a group of super seedy lawyers get together. This group is said to be "supersedeas".

Tort
Derived from the French law, meaning a "wrong".

Verdict
The formal decision rendered by the jury or judge in a trial based on which of the lawyers' lies seemed the most credible.

Voir dire
A fancy French term for interviewing prospective jurors and systematically eliminating anyone with an IQ over 20 from the jury.

Waiver
A client who has given the lawyer his or her money is said to have waived his or her right to ever see the money again. This person is called a waiver, having waved the money good-bye.

Without prejudice
A lawyer who is always willing to take money from anyone and everyone is said to be without prejudice.

Witness
An individual who swears to tell the truth, the whole truth and nothing but the truth and then proceeds to tell the story the way his lawyer instructed him to tell it.

Zero
The amount of money a client has remaining in his or her bank account after being fleeced by the lawyer.

Journospeak

"Journalists aren't supposed to praise things.
It's a violation of work rules almost as serious as buying drinks with our own money or absolving the CIA of something"

P.J. O'Rourke

These are the common clichés and euphemisms used by the journalists and obituary writers

Journalese	**Translation**
Feisty	Short, old female
Flamboyant	Homosexual
Informed source	Reads the daily newspapers
Mega-mogul	Has gone to the top and now currently going to the...
Hot-button issue	Only one to interest the editors
With news wire services	Everything garnered secondhand
Activist	Willingly talks to the press
Dapper	80's fashion reject
Self-styled	'Pseudo-' something
Scandal-plagued	Guilty as hell
Knowledgable observers	The reporter writing the piece and the next desk person
Venerable	By all laws of biology should be dead already
Confirmed bachelor	See 'flamboyant'
Controversial	Has done something bad but can't quite finger him yet
Guru	See 'self-styled'

According to public reports	We were scooped on this one
Embattled	Time to lay down your arms and surrender
War-torn	Can't even find it on a map
Screen legend	Reporter was not even in nappies when this person was a film star
Troubled youth	Arsonist, incendiarist
Scrappy	A runt
Teen idol	Reporter is too old to have heard of him
Beloved	A living icon who's been around for yonks and no one can stand them any more
Petite	Emaciated
Full-figured	Tits of obviously generous proportions
Diminutive	Under five foot tall
Sexy	Better looking than reporter's significant other
Dogged by character issue	Found in bed with floozy
Socialite	Unemployed woman who lives in posh suburb
Effervescent	Verbal diarrhoea
Moderate	Sits on fence, can't commit
Heiress	As in 'socialite' but able to hire a pricey divorce lawyer
Good Samaritan	Too naïve to run away
Innocent bystander	Too slow to run away
Tearful	Well, they could have been tears

Choked up	Definitely might have been tearful
Weeping	One tear about to fall from eyelash
Entrepreneur	Not into Fortune 500 yet but press is helping his case
Mogul	Has made it but press working to change that
Plucky	Someone very young, old, or very short who is still able to walk
Celebrity	Has a publicist
Superstar	Has an agent and a publicist
Modest, well-kept home	The cockroaches anyway seem to be dead
Outspoken	Downright rude man
Strident	Positively rude woman
Exclusive	We were the only ones who returned the spin doctor's calls
Legendary	About to breathe their last
Couldn't be reached for comment	The reporter didn't call outside 9-5
Progressive	Left-wing whacko
Family values	Right-wing whacko
Hero firefighter	He put a fire out
First in the modern history of	No entries on NewsLink
Never	Not in NewsLink OR Google
Hero policeman	Dead policeman
Recently	We lost the press release and don't have details

Mean streets	Slums
Street-wise	Hasn't been hit crossing the road so far
Allegedly	He did it but we can't prove it yet
Shocking revelation	Info leaked on a 'slow news' day
Highly placed source	Someone willing to talk
Prestigious	Indoor loo
Beautiful	Woman savagely murdered
Blonde	See "beautiful"
Reportedly	This bit was plagiarised
Intensely private	Not promoting anything right this minute
Supermodel	Somewhere her picture's been printed
Rarely interviewed	But now promoting something
Source who spoke on condition identity not be revealed	PR spin doctor
Exclusive school/club	Reporter can't gain admittance
Highbrow	A bore
Unclear, uncertain at press time	No one's willing to tell us

Ambiguous Headlines

Ambiguity. What is it? Well it's one of the reasons the writers of computer language have found it very hard to mirror our natural communication. For some reason/s we have found it necessary to keep meaning less than tight and specific. Why? Well maybe it's just to be polite, or because words came from other languages and gave varying nuances or maybe usage developed in different ways across the same language.

However it becomes a problem because of this. If you have a 10 word sentence and each word has three possible interpretations then the formula for possible meanings is: 3x3x3x3x3x3x3x3x3x3 = 59,049 A classical way to demonstrate how ambiguity is a very easy trap to fall into is to give examples from a profession where they directed to avoid ambiguity for obvious reasons. But despite the journalist's first Commandment stating categorically, Thou Shalt not make the headline Ambiguous, it happens with sometimes hilarious double entendres:

Larger Kangaroos Leap Farther, Researchers Find
The Los Angeles Times

Court Rules Boxer Shorts Are Indeed Underwear
Journal of Commerce

Biting Nails Can Be Sign of Tenseness in a Person
The Daily Gazette of Schenectady, New York

Lack of Brains Hinders Research
The Columbus Dispatch

How We Feel About Ourselves is the Core of Self-Esteem, Says author Louise Hart
Boulder, Colorado, Sunday Camera

'Light' Meals are Lower in Fat, Calories
Huntington Herald-Dispatch

Fish Lurk in Streams
Rochester, New York, Democrat & Chronicle

Alcohol Ads Promote Drinking
The Hartford Courant

Malls Try to Attract Shoppers
The Baltimore Sun

Official: Only Rain Will Cure Drought
The Herald-News, Westpost, Massachusetts

Study Finds Sex, Pregnancy Link
Cornell Daily Sun

Survey Finds Dirtier Subways After Cleaning Jobs Were Cut
The New York Times

Whatever Their Motives, Mums Who Kill Kids still Shock Us
—Holland Sentinel

Teenage Girls Often Have Babies Fathered By Men
The Sunday Oregonian

Low Wages Said Key to Poverty
Newsday

Man Shoots Neighbour With Machete
The Miami Herald

Tomatoes Come in Big, Little, Medium Sizes
The Daily Progress, Charlottesville, Virginia

Dirty-Air Cities Far Deadlier Than Clean Ones, Study Shows
The New York Times

Man Run Over by Freight Train Dies
The Los Angeles Times

Scientists See Quakes in L.A. future
The Oregonian

Wachtler Tells Graduates that Life in Jail is Demeaning
The Buffalo News

Free Advice: Bundle up When Out in the Cold
Lexington Herald-Leader

Economist Uses Theory to Explain Economy
Collinsville Herald-Journal

Discoveries: Older Blacks have Edge in Longevity
The Chicago Tribune

Bible Church's Focus is the Bible
Saint Augustine Record, Florida

Clinton Pledges Restraint in Use of Nuclear Weapons
Cedar Rapids

Managers Vs Engineers

Managers with their language are seen to be the spin doctors of corporatism whereas the engineers are perceived as the realists of the business world. See how their language compares

Managerese	**Engineerese**
Ambitious	Unlikely
Aggressive	Very Unlikely
Challenge	Frustration; a dirty job nobody wants
Compatibility	Impossibility
Contribution	Anything a manager likes
Controlled introduction	Let the customer do the CA
Couldn't reach consensus	Total disagreement
Critical path	Something that only a short project can be on
Diagnostics	Something that might give us a clue
Dynamic	Unstable
Elevated to mgt. level	Dead
Encouraged	Ordered
Encouraging process	No tangible results
Exciting	Frightening
Functionally complete	Can do something that appears to work for any feature
Growth opportunity	Learning experience
Helping people	Telling people what to do
Historical	Nobody remembers why
Inappropriate	Stupid (see "Non-optimal" and "Stupid")
Individual contributor	Regular grunt engineer

Interesting	Bear in mind the Chinese curse "May you live in interesting times"
Issue	Problem (see "Opportunity")
Learning experience	Mistake (see "Growth opportunity")
Less than candid	Boldface lie
Leverage	Borrowing someone else's problem
New opportunity	Surprise
Non-optimal	Inappropriate
Opportunity	Problem
Pessimistic	Most likely to occur
Positioning problem	No one will buy it
Power down	Trip over the power-cord
Project transfer	Start project over again
Quality	Japanese; otherwise not well-defined
Redirected	In some contexts: cancelled; otherwise: start again
Resource constrained	Not getting done (see "Time constrained")
Revision	Same software version but from another tape
Richness	Overwhelming complexity
Scenario	Fairy tale
Significantly reduced subset	Castrated
Stable	Stagnant
Strategy	What we tell ourselves we are going to do
Strong personality	Intolerably obnoxious
Strongly encouraged	Ordered on pain of death (see "Encouraged")

Stupid	Incredibly stupid (see "Inappropriate")
Suboptimal	Inappropriate
Tactical plan	What our customers tell us we are going to do
Time constrained	Already too late
Time frame	A period of time in which something will not occur
Transparent change	A change which introduces only subtle problems
We	You

Letters Of Recommendation

How to phrase a letter for an employee when there are certain qualities and characteristics you don't want to lie about but at the same time you are certain these characteristics would count against their candidacy if you spoke too plainly.

For the chronically absent
"A man like him is hard to find."
"It is obvious that he is very time effective."

For the office drunk
"I feel his real talent is wasted here."
"We generally found him loaded with work to do."

For an employee with no ambition:
"He could not care less about the number of hours he had to put in."
"You would indeed be fortunate to get this person to work for you."
"He consistently achieves the standards he sets for himself."

For an employee who is so unproductive that the job is better left unfilled:
"I can assure you that no person would be better for the job."

For an employee who is not worth further consideration as a job candidate:

"I would urge you to waste no time in making this candidate an offer of employment."
"All in all, words fail me in describing how worthwhile a candidate this person would be."

You're called upon for an opinion of a friend who is bone lazy:

"If you get this person to work for you, you will be extremely fortunate."

For a person whose skill count is zero:

"I would have no hesitation in recommending this candidate with no qualifications whatsoever."

For an ex-employee who had problems getting along with fellow workers:

"I am happy to say that this candidate is a former colleague of mine."

For a person with lacklustre credentials:

"All in all, I cannot say enough good things about this candidate or recommend him too highly."

Yes there is a clever use of the double entendre. However, without lying, the person writing the recommendation has not disadvantaged the candidate, and who knows maybe he or she just hasn't found their niche yet. One man's 'job from hell' might be another's ideal job. We must consider that this is a possibility.

Datespeak

"When you are courting a nice girl an hour seems like a second. When you sit on a red-hot cinder a second seems like an hour. That's relativity"

Albert Einstein

Ah the dating scene! That swarming, teeming ocean of humanity, its dreams and yearnings, lust and longing, single (and sometimes not even single) or newly single people in search of...? THE ONE? Well, there could be a number of permutations, fun, companionship, a lover, a lifetime partner. For the unwary it may be useful to know how to decode the terms used in the profiles to avoid disappointment or any nasty surprises.

Euphemism	Translation
40ish	50 plus looking for a 25ish person
Affectionate	Needy, looking for a mother substitute
Ambitious	Ruthless exploiter of others
Appreciates quality	Looking for someone with the cheque book to pay for it
Artist	Unreliable and flighty
Athletic	Watches lots of sport on TV
Beautiful	Spends a lot of time mirror gazing
Disease-free	Had tetanus the last time a dog attacked
Down-to-earth	Petty and pedantic
Educated	Expect to be condescended to
Elegant	Likes to wear jewellery and loves shoes
Employed	Part-time working from home
Enjoy life's pleasures	Over-indulgent, self-centred brat

Enjoy long walks	Car was repossessed some time ago
Enjoy moonlit nights	Can't afford the electricity bill
Excited by life's journey	Haven't got a clue where I'm going
Expressive	Being sued for libel
Fashionably thin	Emaciated to the point of being skeletal
Financially secure	$10 in a savings account and could come into something when uncle dies
Flexible	Desperate
Free spirit	Recreational drug user
Friendship first	As long as it involves being without clothes
Fun loving	Expects to be entertained
Gentle	Hardly able to raise a pulse
Good sense of humour	Laughs at sitcoms on TV
Gourmet cook	Can microwave just about anything
High standards	Blind to one's own failings, unforgiving of others
Honest	I cannot tell the truth
Intuitive	Your opinion counts for nought
Irreverent	Having no idea of social skills
Life of the party	Gets pissed and plays up real fast
Likes to cuddle	Insecure, needing constant reassurance
Marriage-minded	A bigamist looking for another wife
Moody	Manic-depressive
Non-traditional	Get used to meeting the ex-wife who lives downstairs
Old-fashioned	No nudity, lights out and missionary position only

Open-minded	Desperate
Outgoing	A loud mouth
Passionate	Noisy
Perfect	Is completely self-delusional
Physically fit	Life signs
Reliable	Shows up on time, give or take a few hours
Resourceful	Knows who to call when something doesn't work
Self-employed	Not currently possessing a job
Sophisticated	Spends afternoons in Myers browsing through the perfumes and cosmetics
Spiritual	Involved with a cult
Spiritually evolved	Subject to mystical experiences and fainting fits
Spontaneous	Picks his nose at traffic lights, and adjusts his balls at public gatherings
Stylish	Slave to every fashion fad that comes along
Successful	Won $20 in the Lotto once
Sultry/sensual	Easy
Thoughtful	Says please when he wants you to hand him a beer
Unaffected and earthy	A genuine slob with no social skills
Uninhibited	Lacking basic social skills
Very human	With more than one disfiguring deformity
Wants soul mate	Just one step away from being a stalker
Writer	Once when pissed, scribbled a limerick on a beer mat
Youthful	In denial of chronological age

Abbreviations in the personals

SWF, 28, ISO SWM ages NS CP mid-30s, enjoys bike riding, long walks, watching movies and fine dining." What the? Don't worry, help is at hand. Here is the glossary of abbreviations used in personal columns

M	Male	S	Single
F	Female	G	Gay
B	Black	C	Christian
W	White	J	Jewish
H	Hispanic	P	Professional
NA	Native American	N/S	Non-Smoker
A	Asian	N/D	Non-Drinker
WW	Widowed	ISO	In Search Of
D	Divorced	LTR	Long-Term Relationship
BI	Bi-Sexual		
		PT	Petite

Blind Date descriptions decoded

"What is research but a blind date with knowledge?"

Will Harvey

How many men have been talked into meeting a woman the friend says is perfect for him? And how often does the reality fall short of the description? Here they are and what they really mean:

The 'Outdoors Type':
She can shoot straighter than most guys, beat you to the top of the hill running, and take you on in an arm wrestle.

Ready to settle down:
Her biological clock dial is showing five minutes before midnight.

Likes to have a good time:
She gets drunker than a skunk and dances on the counters when she does.

Dandy little housekeeper:
She's been married three times and manages to keep hold of the house each time.

Fine character:
Whatever she did in her past she's reformed now.

Knows how to handle money:
She's great at holding on to her own but has no problem being treated to yours.

Spotless reputation:
And don't anyone in the pub say otherwise.

Strong family ties:
The family is the Family and her father is the Godfather.

Loves children:
She had better, she's pregnant and looking for someone to play daddy to the kid.

Wonderful personality:
Can't really say much about her looks otherwise you'd know I was lying.

Great sense of humour:
She's fat and jolly and will laugh at all your jokes.

Lots of fun at parties:
Often she's the source of mirth.

Mature woman:
She's not handling the aging process too well. Looks older than she really is.

Has the appearance of a young school girl:
Mutton dressed as lamb. A kidult.

Casual:
Dresses like an 80s reject.

Decorated her own place:
No professionals used to help with the job she did on her place—it's a sty.

A great dancer:
She dances topless for a living.

Not overly emotional:
She's down to bursting into tears only ten times a day now.

Doesn't chase men:
No she's more the man-eater, black widow type of predator.

Seldom dates:
She's a closet lesbian who needs arm candy when she goes to events.

Understands men:
She should, she's been around the block enough times.

A good sport:
She knows a great stock of jokes and can drink you under the table.

Looks and dresses like a model:
She's over six foot and weighs forty eight kilos.

Been in show business:
She was in B grade movies once.

Travelled a lot:
She's been in and out of a lot of hotels.

Knows a lot of interesting people:
But none who are prepared to marry her.

Wonderful disposition:
When she doesn't have PMS, that is.

What they say... What they really mean

"Between men and women there is no friendship possible. There is passion, enmity, worship, love, but no friendship."

Oscar Wilde

Men and women, here it is! A quick survival guide for decrypting what those common words and phrases mean when woman talks to man and man talks to woman. Sometimes a single word speaks volumes.

He Says...

Men will have us believe they are simple creatures, that what they say is what they mean. Well except for when they are involved in the military, politics, management or business. However they insist that when it comes to communicating with their significant other they are transparent and quite easy to understand. Well here's a little exercise that demonstrates this may not be entirely true.

What he says	What he really means
I'll think about it	No way, I've forgotten already
It's not you, it's me	It's YOU!
I wanna go to the movies	To make out with you in the dark
We don't have to do anything until you're ready	Woman, put out or get out
I think we should see other people	I already am

I need to get my shit together	I need to stop seeing you so I can see more of her
Honey, I'm home!	Where's my dinner?
You're so lovely when you're mad	I'd rather be f**king you than listening to your rant
I need you	For sex
You're the only girl I've ever cared about	The only girl who hasn't jilted me
I want you back	Well at least for tonight
I miss you so much	I'm very very horny
No honey, of course your bum doesn't look fat in that dress	Oh boy, PMS time again!
Let me do that for you	Before you stuff it up completely
Let me drive	No way am I sitting here for hundreds of kilometres like I get you to do
It's a guy thing	Don't even ask, It's our territory
Good idea	Fat chance! Can't wait to gloat
You expect too much of me	You want me to stay awake!?
I just cut myself. Don't fuss	Even if I severed a limb, the last thing I will do is admit I've hurt myself.
She's a rabid feminist	She won't make my tea
I heard you	I'm hoping that I can fake it with these 3 words because I haven't a clue what you're talking about
I don't need to read the instructions	I'm quite capable to making a mess of it all on my own
"Uh huh", "sure honey" "yes dear"	Pavlov's male response to women's questions when he wants to stay on her good side
Have you lost weight?	I've just done something that's going to require your forgiveness

It would take too long to explain	I haven't got a clue how it works myself
My wife doesn't understand me	She's heard all my stories and is tired of hearing repeats.
We're going to be late	I can drive there like a rally car driver
I WAS listening to you, it's just that I've got a lot on my mind	I was wondering if the blonde over there is wearing a bra
Honey, take a break. You could do with one	I can't hear the game. Turn off the Hoover
That's interesting, dear	So you're still talking, huh
Honey, we don't need material things to prove our love	Oops forgot our anniversary again!
That's women's work	It's dirty, menial and thankless
Will you marry me?	I've run out of food, my friends are moving on and I don't know how to wash my clothes
You know how bad my memory is	I can remember the first girl I ever dated, the registration names and makes of every car I see, and the themes songs for the Westerns but I forgot your birthday.
I was just thinking about you, so I bought you these flowers	I was passing the florist's and the girl selling the flowers gave me the eye
I can't find it	Seeing as it didn't fall into my outstretched hands, I'm clueless to know where to start to look
What do you mean you need new clothes?	I remember you got your last lot only 3 years ago

She says...

Women know how to wax eloquent but sometimes it's the little sigh or the one word which puts either dread or delight into a man's heart. Sometimes men find themselves on the 'wrong side' of their woman because the message she is attempting to convey has passed right over his head. The woman thinks in exasperation "If he loved me he'd know what I wanted without my having to spell it out" and the man's left thinking "If only I had a clue what she means".

What she says	What she really means
I'll be five minutes	Not a literal statement. If you multiply this times five, you won't get frustrated and she won't get irritated that you took her literally
Fine	Argument full stop. Tip: never use this word to describe how a woman looks. You'll start an argument
You want	I want
I'm not upset	Of course I'm upset, you idiot!
You have to learn to communicate	Just agree with me, OK?
I'm not yelling	So what if I am, this is important.
Sure, go ahead	Don't go ahead, if you value your life.
Loud sigh	Even though this isn't strictly a word or phrase it speaks volumes. It is a cue for you to ask what she's upset about. However, don't go there. You won't like it, it's about you.
Soft sigh	For no particular reason known to man, she is, for this moment, content. Don't move a hair or a muscle if you want her to stay in that state.

Nothing.	If you've asked her "What's wrong?" and this is her answer you're in lots of trouble, she will be tight-lipped just waiting to pour out her invective upon you. Lie low!
Thanks	She's thanking you, do not look too deeply into her sincere gratitude.
Thanks a lot	Not the same as "thanks". This means the opposite. She is quite upset by something you've done which is not immediately apparent to you.
We need	I want. After all I decide what we need as I'm more clued into these things than you are.
Do what you want	Yes, go right ahead but pay for it later again and again and again. In other words, if you want a peaceful life do what she wants.
We need to talk	I need to bring up some stuff that is going to sound a whole lot like a whinge
You're so macho	You need to shave and you're sweaty
You're certainly attentive tonight	Sex on your mind, huh?
I'm not emotional and I'm not overreacting	I'm on my period
Be romantic and turn out the lights	So you can't see my flabby thighs
The kitchen is so impractical	I want a whole new house
I really want new curtains	And light fittings, and furniture
Hang the picture there	NO hang it here
I heard a noise	I noticed you were nearly asleep
Do you love me?	Cos I'm going to ask you to prove it by paying for what I want

How much do you love me?	Enough to turn a blind eye on something I did today?
I'll be ready in a minute	Get comfortable, you may be there for a while
Have I got a big butt?	Time to say how beautiful and attractive you find me
Are you listening to me?	If I ask this question it's already too late
No	No
Maybe	No
Yes	No
I'm sorry	You'll be sorry for this
Do you like this recipe?	You had better because it's easy to make and you'll be getting it a lot
Was that the baby?	Up you get and walk him until he goes back to sleep
The dog is barking	Get out there in the rain in your underpants and check it out!
Nothing's wrong	I don't think I need to explain just how wrong everything is
I don't want to talk about it	Don't talk to me, I'm fuming!
What do you think of my new hairstyle	Compliment it or your life won't be worth living
Is she prettier than me?	If you even hesitate in telling me I'm much prettier than her, you will be living in the dog house
Penny for your thoughts	You had better say you were thinking how wonderful I am
I have nothing to wear	Nothing to fit me or nothing that my friends haven't already seen me wearing

I have a headache	Right now I don't want to have anything to do with you let alone get intimate so if you know what's good for you, stay clear
It's a woman's perogative	Payback for the thousands of years of male oppression
Let's make love	I've just finished watching Van Damme in an action movie and I'm pissed enough to pretend you're him
I guess I deserved that	I will not rest until you've paid for my humiliation and getting one up on me
I love you	1) You did something right for a change 2) I did something wrong

Female Prayer

Before I lay me down to sleep,
I pray for a man, who's not a creep,
One who's handsome, smart and strong,
One who loves to listen long,
One who thinks before he speaks,
When he says he'll call, he won't wait weeks.
I pray that he is gainfully employed,
When I spend his cash, won't be annoyed.
Pulls out my chair and opens my door,
Massages my back and begs to do more.
Oh! Send me a man who'll make love to my mind,
Knows what to answer to "How big's my behind?"
I pray that this man will love me to no end,
And never attempt to hit on my friend.
And as I kneel and pray by my bed,
I look at the creep you sent me instead.

Amen.

Male Prayer

I pray for a rich, deaf-mute nymphomaniac with huge boobs who owns a liquor store.

Amen

Dictionary of Evaluation Comments

"Criticism may not be agreeable, but it is necessary. It fulfils the same function as pain in the human body. It calls attention to an unhealthy state of things."

Winston Churchill

Some amongst you may be curious to decipher what the supervisor is really saying in all those employee work performance evaluations s/he keeps cranking out.

Average:
Two bricks short of a pallet

Exceptionally well qualified:
So far no detectable boo boos

Active socially:
Drinks like a sea horse

Zealous attitude:
Full of one's own opinions

Character above reproach:
Still legal until detected

Unlimited potential:
Will stay with the firm through thick and thin till retirement

Quick thinking:
Thinks on his feet when it comes to explaining away errors

Takes pride in work:
Full of himself

Takes advantage of every opportunity to progress:
Sucks up to superiors by offering free drinks etc

Indifferent to instruction:
Actually knows more than superiors

Stern disciplinarian:
Boring, overbearing bully

Tactful in dealing with superiors:
Knows when to zip the lips

Approaches difficult problems with logic:
Knows how to delegate the tough ones

A keen analyst:
Doesn't know his way out of a paper bag

Not a desk person:
Didn't go to Uni

Expresses self well:
Can string two simple sentences together

Spends extra hours on the job:
Nothing to go home to

Conscientious and careful:
S**t scared

Meticulous in attention to detail:
A pedantic nitpicker

Demonstrates qualities of leadership:
Has a loud strident voice

Judgement is usually sound:
Just born lucky

Maintains professional attitude:
An elitist snob

Keen sense of humour:
Knows a heap of whiffy jokes

Strong adherence to principles:
As immovable as an elephant in a mud puddle

Gets along extremely well with superiors and subordinates alike:
No backbone, wants to please everyone

Slightly below average:
Three wildebeest short of a herd

Of great value to the organisation:
Manages to get stuff in on deadline

Is unusually loyal:
Nowhere else to go

Alert to company developments:
Very attuned to office politics

Requires work-value attitudinal readjustment:
Lazy old fart and stubborn as a donkey

Hard worker:
Doesn't know the easy way to get things done

Enjoys job:
Not enough to do to take that grin off his face

Happy:
Obviously earning more than he can spend

Well organised:
Does too much of the busy work

Competent:
Despite the 'help' of a supervisor can still get work done

Consults with supervisor often:
Suck up pain in the arse

Will go far:
Nepotism at work

Should go far:
Yes please, only if the evaluator bribed or talking about a relative

Uses time effectively:
Works by the clock

Very creative:
Finds a dozen or two dozen ways to do anything, but nothing original

Uses resources well:
Able to delegate everything

Deserves promotion:
Company to create new job title to keep this worker energised/ motivated

Eduspeak

"Education... has produced a vast population able to read but unable to distinguish what is worth reading."

G. M. Trevelyan

What teachers, educators or knowledge consultants write on the reports about their students and what they really mean. Saying anything defamatory about little Jessie or Bessie could bring down the wrath of the empowered caregivers.

Teacher/Educator writes	Translation is
Jane demonstrates problems with spatial relationships	Hasn't found her locker yet
Jessie exhibits exceptional verbal skills and an obvious propensity for social interaction	She never stops talking
Paul's leadership qualities need to be more democratically directed	He's a bully
Jonathan accomplishes tasks when his interest is frequently stimulated	He has the attention span of a gnat

Donald is making progress in learning to express himself respectfully	He no longer uses vulgarities when talking back to me
Alfred demonstrates some difficulty meeting the challenges of information retention	He'd forget his name if it wasn't taped to his desk
Bunny needs encouragement in learning to form lasting friendships	Nobody likes her
Kenny is working toward grade level	He may even reach it, next year
Joel appears to be aware of all classroom activities	He just can't focus on the one we're involved in
Brad seems to have difficulty distinguishing between fact and fantasy	He lies like a rug
Allie enjoys dramatisation. She may be headed for a career in show business	Ringling Bros. and Barnum & Bailey Circus comes to mind
Takira's creative writing skills are reminiscent of Socrates	It's all Greek to me
Eleanor is a creative problem solver	She hasn't gotten an answer right yet
Jack demonstrates an avid interest in recreational reading	He "recreates" while other students read
Mary appears to be showing an increased desire to consider demonstrating acceptable classroom behaviour	She now appears to know the classroom rules. Some day she may even obey one
Pablo participates enthusiastically in all art activities	He's especially adept at throwing pottery, and paint, and...
Jeremy is stimulated by participation in sequential activities	He consistently insists on fighting his way to the front of the recess line
Juanita needs more home study time	Could you please keep her home more often?

Michael demonstrates a need for guidance in the appropriate use of time	Three hours a day is entirely too much time to spend picking his nose
David frequently appears bored and restless. You might want to consider placing him in a more challenging environment	Prison, perhaps?

Lost in truncation

"DNA is an abbreviation for deoxyribonucleicantidisestablishmentarianism, a complex string of syllables."

Dave Barry

SMS: The abbreviated language of the mobile phone devotees and the Instant Messenger users on the Net who also utilize elements of it, there is now officially another addiction we can fall foul of, SMS addiction. Cities in the US have been set up to deal with this serious obsession. Some users have been known to send as many as 70-100 messages per day. It's a wonder they don't get RSI of the digits. What effect will abbreviating words have on the richness of our language? What if your latest squeeze sent you this message?

"ILuvU Alwz&4evr"

Would it fill you with delight? Would it mean the same as "I love you always and forever" or would you say it had lost something in truncation?

AFAIK	As far as I know
AFK	Away from keyboard
Alwz	Always
ASL	Age, sex, location
ASAP	As soon as possible
ATB	All the best
ATK	At the keyboard
ATM	At the moment

A3	Anytime, anywhere, anyplace
B	Be
B4	Before
BAK	Back at keyboard
BBL	Be back later
BBS	Be back soon
BCNU	Be seeing you
BF	Boyfriend
BFN/B4N	Bye for now
BFz4evr	Best friends forever
BHL8	Be home late
BIL	Boss is listening
BN	Been
BOL	Best of luck
BRB	Be right back
BRBGP	Be right back gotta pee
BRT	Be right there
BTW	By the way
C	See
CU	See you
CUB L8R	Call you back later
CU@	See you at
CUL	See you later
CYA	See you around, see ya
CMi	Call me
CMON	Come On
CUB L8R	Call you back later
CUL8R	See you later
CYR BOS	Call your boss
CYR BRO	Call your brother
CYR H	Call your husband
CYR MA	Call your mother
CYR OFIS	Call your office
CYR PA	Call your father
CYR SIS	Call your sister
CYR WF	Call your wife
Dk	Don't know

DNR	Dinner
doN	Doing
Dur?	Do you remember
E2eg	Ear to ear grin
EOD	End of discussion
EOL	End of lecture
EVRY1	Everyone
EZY	Easy
EZ	Easy
FAQ	Frequently asked questions
FC	Fingers crossed
F2F	Face-to-face
F2T	Free to talk
F?	Friends?
FITB	Fill in the blank
FOMCL	Fell out of my chair laughing
FYEO	For your eyes only
FYA	For your amusement
FYI	For your information
F2T	Free to talk
GAL	Get a life
GF	Girlfirend
GG	Good game
GMeSumLuvin	Give me some lovin'!
GMTA	Great minds think alike
GR8	Great!
GSOH	Good salary, own home
GTSY	Glad to see you
GUDLUK	Good luck
G9	Genius
H2cus	Hope to see you soon
H8	Hate
HAGN	Have a good night
HAND	Have a nice day
HldMeCls	Hold me close
HRU	How are you?
Ht4U	Hot for you

HTH	Hope that helps
H&K	Hugs and kisses
IAC	In any case
IAD8	It's a date
IC	I see
ICQ	A chat program: icq.com
IDK	I don't know
IGotUBabe	I've got you babe
IIRC	If I recall correctly
ILU	I love you
ILU2	I love you too
ILUA	I love you alot
ILuvU Alwz&4evr	I love you always and forever
IMO	In my opinion
IMHO	In my honest (or humble) opinion
IMBLuv	It must be love
IMI	I mean it
IMO	In my opinion
IMTNG	I am in a meeting
IM 4 U	I am for you
Im :) 2hv Mt U	I'm happy to have met you
IOU	I owe you
IOW	In other words
IRL	In real life
Its F8	It's fate
IUSS	If you say so
IYD	In your dreams
IYKWIM	If you know what I mean
J4F	Just for fun
JFK	Just for kicks
JK	Just kidding
JHB	Johannesburg
JstCllMe	Just call me
KC	Keep cool
KHUF	Know how you feel
KISS	Keep it simple, stupid
KIT	Keep in touch
KOTC	Kiss on the cheek

KOTL	Kiss on the lips
L&N	Landing
LDR	Long distance relationship
LMAO	Laugh my arse off
LOL	Laughing out loud
LDN	London
LSKOL	Long slow kiss on the lips
LTNC	Long time no see
LUV	Love
LtsGt2gthr	Let's get together
lyN	Lying
L8	Late
L8r	Later
MTE	My thoughts exactly
M$ULkeCrZ	Miss you like crazy!
MC	Merry Christmas
MGB	May God bless
Mob	Mobile
MU	Miss you
MUSM	Miss you so much
MTE	My thoughts exactly
MYOB	Mind your own business
M8	Mate
NRN	No reply necessary
NA	No access
NC	No comment
NE	Any
NE1	Anyone
NITING	Anything
No1	No one
NP	No problem
nufN	Nothing
NWO	No way out
OIC	Oh, I see
OTOH	On the other hand
O4U	Only for you
PCM	Please call me

PCME	Please call me
PITA	Pain in the arse
pl&	Planned
PLS	Please
PLZ 4GV ME	Please forgive me
PML	Piss myself laughing
po$bl	Possible
PRT	Party
PRW	Parents are watching
PTB	Please text back
PUKS	Pick Up Kids
QPSA?	Que pasa? (what's happening?)
QT	Cutie
T+	Think positive
TDTU	Totally devoted to you
Thx	Thanks
TIC	Tongue in Cheek
Tks	Thanks
TMIY	Take me I'm yours
THNQ	Thank you
TIA	Thanks in advance
TLA	Three letter acronym
TTFN	Ta ta for now.
TTYL	Talk to you later
TUL	Tell you later
T2Go	Time to go
T2ul	Talk to you later
U	You
U2	You too
UI!	You idiot!
UR	You are
uvbnsmuchd	You've been smooched
URT1	You are the one
UR TH WKEST LNK GDBY	You are the weakest link, goodbye
UR4Me	You are for me
U4E	Yours forever

VRI	Very
W@	What
W8N	Waiting
WAN2	Want to
Wan2 C a moV?	Want to see a movie?
WB	Welcome back
WOT	What
WRT	With respect to
WRU	Where are you?
WTF	What the f**k?
WTH	What the hell
WTG	Way to go!
WTMPI	Way Too much personal information
WUF	Where are You from?
WUWH	Wish you were here
W4u	Waiting for you
W8	Wait
W84M	Wait for me
X!	Typical woman
X	Kiss
XO	Kiss and a hug
XclusvlyUrs	Exclusively yours
XLNT	Excellent
Y	Why?
Y!	Typical man
YBS	You'll be sorry
YGM	You got mail
YR	Your
ZZZZZ	Sleeping

Contradictory sayings

"I believe that truth has only one face:
that of a violent contradiction."

Georges Bataille

Here could lie the key to what constitutes the truth, how can you have contradictory aphorisms, both of which can be considered the most apt in context? Nevertheless, here are some examples:

Nothing ventured, nothing gained	Better safe than sorry
What's good for the goose is good for the gander	One man's meat is another man's poison
He who hesitates is lost	Look before you leap
Forewarned is forearmed	Cross your bridges when you come to them
Out of the mouths of babes come all wise sayings	With age comes wisdom
The bigger, the better	The best things come in small packages
The pen is mightier than the sword	Actions speak louder than words
Don't judge a book by its cover	Clothes make the man
Many hands make light work	Too many cooks spoil the broth
Out of sight, out of mind	Absence makes the heart grow fonder
Life is what you make it	What will be, will be
Two's company; three's a crowd	The more, the merrier
Beware of Greeks bearing gifts	Never look a gift horse in the mouth
Nothing ventured, nothing gained	Fools rush in where angels fear to tread

If at first you don't succeed
try try try again

Don't go beating your
head up against a brick
wall

Curiosity killed the cat

Seek and you shall find

Fools never differ

Great minds think alike

The squeaky wheel gets the grease

Silence is golden

Tomorrow will take care of itself

Save for a rainy day

A setting hen never lays

A rolling stone gathers
no moss

Remember When...

A computer was something on TV
from a science fiction show of note
A window was something you hated to clean
and ram was the cousin of a goat

Meg was the name of my girlfriend
and gig was a job for the nights
Now they all mean different things
and that really mega bytes

An application was for employment
A program was a TV show
A cursor used profanity
A keyboard was a piano

Memory was something that you lost with age
A CD was a bank account
And if you had a 3″ floppy
you hoped nobody found out

Compress was something you did to the garbage
Not something you did to a file

And if you unzipped anything in public
you'd be in jail for awhile

Log on was adding wood to the fire
Hard drive was a long trip on the road
A mouse pad was where a mouse lived
And a backup happened in your commode

Cut you did with a pocket knife
Paste you did with glue
A web site was a spider's home
and a virus was the flu

I guess I'll stick to my pad and paper
And the memory in my head
I hear nobody's been killed in a computer crash
But when it happens they wish they were dead

Tech Speak

This is only a smattering of the coined terms that have sprung up around the world of computers, the Internet and associated hard and software.

Blog
It's a website that keeps being updated with chronological material, like an online diary. Blogs are all the rage. They represent that person's own online "soap box".

Cyberchondriacs
Those surfers of the medical websites obsessively searching for symptoms of diseases which they can use to explain their latest malaise.

Cryptonoia
A paranoia which reads a hidden meaning into every code.

Cybergriping
Having a whinge on a website especially designed to absorb gripes.

Cyberskeptics
These are a growing group of legal people who think it's crazy to be creating a whole set of "cyberlaws" for the Net when they believe that the law of the real world is as valid.

Dot.commie
There's a Luddite movement sweeping the world. There are those who will have nothing more to do with the Dot.com world but insist on face-to-face, hand-to-eye, human interactions.

Drive-by download
Beware! This is one of those insidious sites that downloads onto your computer automatically often without your consent.

Dub-dub-dub
It's short for www and is a favourite of the techies when ringing through the Net address of a site.

Evergreening
A process of keeping your web page content current, up-to-date and relevant.

Dot Con Artist
Someone who's an internet scam artist.

Ego surfing
When you can't resist surfing the Web for references to yourself and what others are saying about you. Of course you either have to have done something worthy of celebrity or else some notoriety. Or maybe you posted some poems on a poetry website.

Etherface
When your only connection to another person is exclusively via email, this is the term you use.

Fritterware
Software with a whole load of excess capabilities which are irresistible to use and don't really add anything to productivity. It's also used for software that employees use whenever the boss isn't watching.

Generation C
This represents the growing group of consumers of the Net who insist on creating their very own "content". Pics taken off digital cameras, and ephemera, makes for a hotch-potch. They make up their own blogs.

Generation D
Whether you're 7 or 77, if you're completely at ease with the digital revolution then you're part of Generation D(igital)

Get-Rich-Click
This relates to people who believe they'll be able to amass a fortune through internet investments, or else by setting up an online business.

Googling
Named after the Google (www.google.com) search engine. "I'll google that name and see if they have any track history"

Handraulics
The manual process.

Hit-and-run-page
This refers to a web page which receives a ginormous number of hits but disappears about a week later. Most of these sites contain pornographic material and are shut down once the administrators have sussed why their network is suddenly in a "traffic snarl of the Information Superhighway".

Jitterati
Generation D(igital) gets jittery after sipping one too many cups of coffee.

Knee-mail
This is religion's attempt to get with the new information email capabilities.

Phishing
This is the scam of making a replica web page in order to fool the user and garner their personal, financial or password details.

Pierre Salinger Syndrome
It's the tendency for online users, especially the novices, to assume that anything published on the net is automatically true.

Sextuple-u
This is just another way of pronouncing the "www" at the beginning of net addresses.

Sneezers
These are people who help spread "idea viruses" or memes: the latest book they enthuse about that others go out to buy or rave about a new brand of peanut butter.

12:00 Flasher
A person who is challenged by complex technology, a luddite, the giveaway being that the VCR continually flashes "12.00".

Yetties
Young Entrepreneurial, tech-based twenty-somethings. The digital generation who are au fait with living the high tech jet set existence.

YYSSW
The Y generation have their own text messaging shorthand "Yeah, yeah, sure, sure, whatever".

Web Rage
The kind of pent-up frustrations that dealings with the www world inspire. Slow downloads, non-existent links or information hard to track down.

Property Speak

Have you ever been taken in by a house ad you circled in the classifieds? It was a description of your dream home and you openly drooled. You rushed to the phone to arrange an appointment with the agent, so happy that it had not yet been sold. You grabbed the spouse and went off, babbling nearly incoherently about your future residence.

Oh, but then you saw the house supposedly described in the property ad, and you were gob-smacked at how words can be so elastic in their ability to stretch the truth. Well this section's for you prospective house buyers, so that you may know the tricks of euphemism and distortion.

Location! Location! Location!
Right across from a school or else a bus terminal.

Security System
Neighbour has a dog.

Needs TLC
Needs building from the ground up.

Updated Kitchen
The sink is now draining water and the taps don't leak any more.

Motivated Seller
Has been on the market for 7 years, and the vendor is getting desperate for a good reason.

Convenient
Located on freeway entrance ramp.

Mint
Someone has spilled spearmint mouthwash all over the carpet.

Neutral Decor
No strong purples or oranges but the walls are a shade of brown. The half way through the winter tan look.

Move-in condition
Front door missing.

Sophisticated city living
Right next to a singing pub.

Old-world charm
Has some woodwork, needs cleaning.

Contemporary feeling
Has no woodwork, needs cleaning.

Close to lakes
Parking may pose a problem in the touristy months.

Wide open floor plan
Previous owner removed the structural indoor supporting walls. You may need to get in an engineer.

Cosy
No room larger than 9 x 6.

Lower-level family room
Ping-pong table over sewer opening.

Light open spaces
Many holes in walls and ceiling.

Outstanding
Outrageously painted in colours that make it stand out like a sore thumb.

A wealth of period features
Dry rot, rising damp and an electrical circuit best operated in rubber gloves and wellies.

Box room
Great for storage if you manage to collapse the one or two boxes before you put them away.

By private treaty
If it went to auction it would never reach the reserve price.

Compact
You wouldn't swing a mouse in that space.

Country Gentleman's Residence
No longer suitable for agricultural tenants.

Deceptive appearance
It looks shocking.

Delightful rural location
In the flight path of an Air Force Base that flies test jets.

Easily maintained
Only if you have hired help, that is.

Extensively Modernised
Former DIY owner had a breakdown under the strain.

For the gardening enthusiast
More like a jungle.

Local authority grants available
About to be condemned.

Much sought after
Wishful thinking. The two times it's been on the market it hasn't been snapped up.

Owner eager to sell
If it goes within a week the subsidence cracks won't be noticed.

Partial central heating
When the sun shines through the windows in summer.

Period residence
Built in the last several years.

Quiet, secluded setting
Close to a cemetery

Rare opportunity to buy
No one else wants it.

Select neighbourhood
Next door to a sewage treatment works

Sold
But only until vendor gets better offer.

Subject to new instructions
They've just discovered concrete cancer.

Unspoiled
Planning permission granted for field next door.

Unusual features
Roof-free.

Unusual location
In the path of a projected motorway.

Useful outbuildings
No inside dunny.

Well situated
The neighbours get a great view of your back yard.

Within easy distance of
Next door to a pub and opposite a sex shop.

Truspeak

Truspeak. My term to describe coined words that tell it how it is; words, that by combining terms indicate that there is a blurring between ideas or elements; that there is an ambiguity; that this is our current reality.

Often they are quite humorous in this strange upside down world of the early millennium, what some would call the Post-Truth Era, one could say:

"Humour is the last refuge of the politically incorrect."

Humour is no respecter of taboos and sacred cows, no conformist to our more delicate sensitivities, or humour was before the reign of manipulation and deception. The court jester in the court of the autocratic monarch did not have his head severed from his body whilst poking fun at all things monarchical. Parody and satire was a way of providing a true reflection of the realities of courtly existence.

Humour is the antidote to manipulation and mass control. There is so much that is ludicrous and comical about the tools utilised to make us do what they "want" us to do, once they are deconstructed, whether it's buying product fantastic-you-have-to-have-one, or approving of warmongering based on a spin, being scammed into believing a scheme will make you Ali-baba fabulously rich.

Examples of Truspeak are:

Desktitute
To be gainfully employed but without a working-space, sometimes temporary and part of a natural cycle, sometimes endemic to a corporation.

Feetlips
Where foot ends up in mouth very often, so often that it warrants this label. That person's unerring ability to speak first and think later.

E-judicate
Screening the wheat from the chaff on the Internet.

Neospeak

Here it is, a celebration and explanation of these new words.

Bamble
A cross between babbling and rambling. Not as relaxed as rambling, but not as frantic as babbling. Example: "Dear readers, when I last left you to bamble on, as I do, am doing, Gina and I were just being attacked by a French ruffian."

Bobbleheading
Like daisies in a spring field all nodding their heads to the passing breeze, this is the concerted and unanimous nodding behaviour of executives around the boardroom, attendees at the evangelist's happening and other species of "Yes-preferenced" folk.

Boozled
Sozzled, legless, can't walk the straight line, more parts alcohol than blood.

Boinkbackability
Resilience, that Tigger-like quality where the more life pushes you down the further you bounce heavenwards.

Cameraholic
To be in love with the camera, the image it produces of making videos. You see them here, you see them there, they go through life behind the lens.

Celebrify
It's the capacity to make someone or something a star.

Cinemetiquette
The unspoken rules of watching a movie in a public place. No-Nos being leaving the cell phone on; laughing or screaming in horror at inappropriate times; divulging the plot before the crunch comes or chattering as the movie unfolds, or taking in very noisy food packaging.

Craptastic
A merge of crappy + fantastic which speaks volumes for our current lifestyles, how we can be in awe of what is quite dreadful.

Crockumentary
Call it a 'crockumentary' when you believe this piece of film footage leans more to propaganda than to factual reporting.

Cyberbully
Someone who harasses and harangues others on the Information Superhighway, the 'road rage' equivalent is the driver with his hand on the horn and his head out the window shouting expletives to all and sundry.

Desktitute
To be gainfully employed but without a working-space: sometimes temporary and part of a natural cycle—sometimes endemic to a corporation.

Disgustalicious
The contradictory capacity for a thing to be both disgusting and delicious at the same time. For example fast food can at one level make the mouth water but at the rational level be quite disgustingly unhealthy, greasy and full of fat and sugar.

Dumbdowning
Any behaviour, action, message, belief that acts to bring homo sapiens a little further away from the species capacity for complex thought and interpretation.

Earwitness
This is the aural counterpart to the 'eyewitness'—the eavesdropper, the chance passerby, the person sitting in the pub who overhears a conversation between two criminals about robbing the local store but doesn't get to see their faces.

E- judicate
Being able to screen what is and isn't true or real on the internet.

E-Quaintance
A cyber pal, someone out there in the ether of cyberspace whom one has no particular desire to know as a real person in 3D.

E-Static
The emotional condition of a person when they believe they have met their soul mate online. Unfortunately upon further acquaintance the condition evaporates like mist on water.

Euphemise
To insult someone by using one or more euphemisms.

Everydayality
The ho-hum common variety kind of stuff one encounters every day.

Exotigrotti
A combination of something that is both exotic and yet not quite to one's taste as yet e.g. the way one might feel about blue vein cheese at first acquaintance.

Exverbicate
Removing certain words or concepts from a language in order to limit thought; banning books; censorship of words which are considered beyond the pale; political correctness is guilty of exverbication.

Fadtastic
This expression can be used for the latest rage or vogue in video games, shoes or MTV songster.

Fahoodled
Juggling too many thought bubbles in the air, with the result that some fall and burst upon impact.

Feetlips
Where foot ends up in mouth very often, so often that it warrants this nomer. That person's unerring ability to speak first and think later.

Ficto-facto
A kind of factual fictitious account of something maybe on a par with the literary Faction.

Fittening
The ability of some activity to increase fitness incrementally, "running up those stairs ten times a day is very fittening".

Flabgasted
Catching one's reflection in the mirror when no clothes have been thrown on and finding with shock and horror that the thighs, hips and belly have been overtaken by 'flab'.

Flastname
A convention for identity very popular in email addresses especially in corporations where the first initial is combined with the last name. So Joe Bloggs is Jbloggs@fahoozey.com

Flimflamjam
A condition produced by telling a lie which leads to more lies which leads to the liar not remembering what they might have said in the past.

Flooming
Temper flaring, frothing at the mouth, fuming with rage, get the picture?

Floordrobe
This is what many tweenagers have instead of that space where clothes actually hang vertically, this is the wall-to-wall look where the clothing is strewn horizontally and may well stay in that state for some time.

Flusterpated
Have you ever felt so flustered that you lost the power of speech and felt paralysed? Well you were 'flusterpated'.

Frenemy
The kind of people in our circle of friends who seem to find many inventive ways to sabotage one's style and self-worth, only it's done under the camouflage of 'what's best for you'.

Froogle
Being frugal when using 'google' the search engine.

Fumb
It deserves a name of its own, the big toe. Not enough attention is given to this paragon of usefulness standing sentinel every day of our lives, not afraid to stand shoulder to shoulder with the lesser digital toe-mortals.

Girafitti
Vandalism spray-painted very, very high.

Glamazon
The glamour of Amazons, greek gods and bronzed bodies—for instance Troy the movie and its heroes.

Gobsmacked
Utterly shocked; more than flabbergasted; completely taken by surprise, the mouth forming a perfect O in stupefaction.

Gruntled
The antonym of 'disgruntled' so it means contented.

Guppygoth
Someone who wears their own brand of uniform in order to conform to a subculture, refers in particular to 'gothic culture'—the white-faced, black dressing kind.

Hatriot
Someone whose patriotism is more parts hate of those not of his country than love of his country.

Headwhine
A newspaper headline that has a nagging element to it.

Hippycrite
The children of the revolution who wore flowers in the long locks, fought for all kinds of causes in the 60's and 70's but who with the advancing of years have moved to quite different ground, they might even claim that they never 'inhaled' any of that culture.

Hypnocrapso
A play on 'ipso facto' this is a term for knowing you're being manipulated but feeling so mesmerized that you simply can't resist. 'That TV ad was so hypnocrapso'.

Hugemongous
Larger than large. 'Godzilla was hugemongous.'

Hugmuggler
Someone who is affectionate and likes to hug. A merger of both the hug + muggle which is a derivative of the very popular Harry

Potter books by J K Rowling which characterise ordinary mortals as muggles. So you hugmuggle when you hug one of these.

Ignoranus
Someone who has the ability to combine stupidity with being an arsehole.

Infoganda
This is propaganda dressed up as factual news reporting. It has an inclination to spread across all kinds of media.

Intaxication
The elation and intoxication of getting a tax refund cheque, as opposed to having to give them something back.

-ish
1.) to approximate a time of arrival or departure: "'Could you arrive at around four?' he ished." 2.) To arrive or depart at approximately the correct time: "He ishes all the time! He arrived at 5:15 when I told him to be there at 5 o'clock."

IYKWIM
Abbreviation for "If you know what I mean."

Jamais Vu
The bizarre sense that something very common is new and foreign. This can happen, for example, if one says a very common word like "what" or "must" over and over and over again.

Kidult
An adult still in touch with their inner child to the point where they would rather prioritise fun and indulgence to any of the more sober adult pursuits.

Legitimake
Making something licit or legal.

Loofproof
This is the kind of thing that is very hard to make foolproof because it is very subject to misinterpretation and open to ambiguity.

Ludelicious
An image or nuance which is both slightly obscene but also uncommonly appealing.

Maggels paradox
Nothing is new under the sun. Having googled what you thought was a radical idea, you find that it has already occurred to a number of others.

Manipulatrix
A female who has made an art form out of emotional manipulation.

Mcjob
The proletariat job of the workforce requiring little skill, and receiving poor remuneration. Such positions are to be found in the fast food industry.

Mobisode
An episode in a long running gangster TV series such as Sopranos; or a brief taster of a programme which can be viewed on a mobile phone.

Mockumentary
This is a fictional film styled in the form of a documentary. It does not however pretend to be factual.

Moralgasm
An ecstatic fit of self-righteous preaching. Example: "Overhearing two older men on the bus whispering quietly about how it was a mistake to grant women the right to vote brought Julia to moralgasm."

Nerdly
Nerdy, but in a cool, hip, "Hackers"/"Matrix" sort of way. Similar in meaning to geek chic.

Netaholic
Someone addicted to all things nettish. A fascination with engaging in cyberspace activities.

Nibling
Nieces and nephews. "My brother has three kids, so I have three niblings".

Nostradamisma
The inclination to believe that everything has been foretold by Nostradamus however this is generally demonstrated using hindsight.

Nounification
The increasing creep in the English language towards making nouns of verbs. This has the effect of giving language a passive voice which effectively takes accountability away from the 'subject'. If a politician makes a statement, rather than stating, it removes him from being associated actively with the stating. There is a great deal of this kind of language distortion happening with bullet pointing in presentations and unfortunately it is now creeping into primary schools.

Patheticism
A thing that is extremely pathetic.

Pedlock
A pedestrian traffic jam.

Peevert
Someone with the uncanny ability to peeve others.

Phonecrastinate
Avoiding answering the phone and waiting for the number to display in case it's a telemarketer, a disgruntled ex-lover or the debt collector.

Povertarian
A nice euphemism for someone steeped in poverty.

Prebuttal
Preemptive + rebuttal. The rebuttal is made even before the claims needing rebuttal have been made. A bit like putting away the plates before the meal is even served up.

Premercial
Pre + commercial a blend. You're waiting for your computer to load the website you've requested and up jumps an ad.

Presenteeism
Being present at work when you're sick which many workers find they need to do. However it has been discovered that this can be very damaging to productivity because anything communicable spreads through air conditioning systems causing many workers to feel under par.

Procrasturbate
Delaying simply because for you, putting things off feels deliciously naughty; or masturbating as a way of delaying having to do things on the to-do list.

Prop-agenda
This is not the control of our thoughts, but the control of the kinds of things we think about.

Pythonesque
From those crazy bizarre fantastical Monty Python days, this is the adjective to describe anything that satisfies those criteria.

Quackupuncture
A person posing as a genuine acupuncturist who is simply a charlatan.

Quinquennian
Someone living today who looks as though they stepped out of the 1950s; a 1950's reject, hair, clothes, style.

Refreezerate
Putting the defrosted food back into the freezer causing it to change from its original condition.

Residrool
That little puddle of saliva on your pillow (or school desk) after having slept for some time with your mouth open.

Respectacle
Looking respectable because one is wearing spectacles and isn't expected to do anything surprising or amusing. Blondes are known to wear eyeglasses to belie their reputation for being light on intellect.

Rumorazzi
Rumour a la paparazzi, the celebrity chasers.

Sabottical
A vacation spent doing some serious drinking.

Satiscraptory
Just adequate standard even though it is poor. Some hotels could be considered satiscraptory.

Scanxious
Anxious prior to a scan (CAT, MRI, CT, etc.) for some kind of disease or malignancy.

Scribulate
Waking up in the middle of the night with an idea and writing it down feverishly on a notepad by your bedside. Finding in the morning that it's incredibly hard to decipher.

Sekuhara
The short form for 'sexual harassment' but it has a Japanese flavour to it.

Sheeple
This is a newly coined term for the herd, people who are content to follow the lead without indulging in critical thought because it's all too hard.

Shopaholic
A person who is addicted to shopping and fun.

Shizzledizz
When something is 'shizzledizz' then you think it's appealing.

Signother
Whoever is your 'main squeeze'.

Slanguage
This is language and jargon that is used exclusively for a particular sub-culture.

Sliminazi
Like a reformed smoker's fascism, this person is on a diet which is working and they're giving a blow-by-blow account and tyrannising those who aren't doing anything about their weight.

Smarterang
The person who gets smarter by osmosis. They rub shoulders and interact with smarter people and hey presto! Their IQ goes up a few notches.

Snowoptimist
A person who loves snow, and always believes it will fall (especially to give a White Christmas).

Stalkerazzi
Paparazzi who are willing to engage in stalking, high-speed chases or otherwise aggressive and harassing behaviour to get pictures of Hollywood pop or movie stars. This behaviour seems to have arisen as newspapers try to avoid the increasingly exorbitant royalties required by pop and movie stars to be photographed.

Starchitect
The star architect in a firm.

Swabble
To both sway and wobble.

To-don't list
A list of tasks that never seem to get done.

Totoiletarianist
One who adheres to and insists upon a system of strict rules over how the toilet is used (e.g. insisting the toilet seat should be down after each usage).

Toyetic
This is a blend of toy + etic (that little suffix employed to make an adjective out of a noun) the kind of products which can easily be made to accessorise a film e.g. action figures as with Star Wars and Spiderman, which of course multiplies profits for the filmmakers.

Trustifarian
An individual from relatively affluent, often Caucasian background, that adopts the superficial trappings of Jamaican culture.

Unsackable
Unable to be sacked, having a job for life no matter what mistakes are made or what incompetence is demonstrated.

Vacademic
A person with a wealth of knowledge or expertise about a subject of little or no value or significance.

Vidiot
Persons who buy new-fangled devices such as VCRs and DVD players and cameras but who lack the ability to do much more

than operate the on-and-off button. I suspect there are quite a few vidiots out there.

Wackademia
The study of strange new-agey or old world phenomena. UFOs, crop circles, Egyptology etc.

Wallowism
Here's the antonym to escapism. Instead of escaping the woes of the world and one's own hapless state, the wallowist immerses himself in woebegoneness.

Wimble
Starting out strongly but eventually running out of puff. As seen on centre court at Wimbledon in more than one tennis match.

Wurfing
Surfing the internet at work and realising that it could be construed as being for work purposes.

Witburst
Suddenly coming up with a good idea, or erupting with a turn of phrase which is considered by others to be quite witty.

Yesnaby
A yes combined with a maybe = no, not now, and maybe never.

Zlander
Denigrating or insulting someone in your sleep. You will hear about it in the morning if the object of your zlander is the person you share the bed with!

Yumeriffic
Deliciously wonderful.

Zonk out
To fall so fast asleep as to be almost comatose.

Hetera-Metra-Tetra-Sexual

Here are some newly coined words to reflect our current gender realities. The terms give a depiction of life in the first part of the new millennium.

Arm candy
The visually excellent person who accompanies a man or woman to event or a party, on their arm but who is often not romantically involved with them.

Beautality
Using beauty as a weapon against your peers and enemies. Or else surround yourself with beautiful people and unarm the ones you want to defeat.

Castracise
To combine castration with ostracism, a technique skilfully employed by some women when wanting to stop a man dead in his tracks.

Cellular Interruptus
Cell phone does its zing-zing-zing or whatever ditty it is configured for and the owner stops in the middle of flagrante delecte to take the call. A major insult for his partner-in-sex!

Chica-in-charge,
Opposite of "damsel in distress". A girl or woman who acts with inner strength, courage, and calm yet quick thought in a dangerous situation, and often leads her own rescue effort. You could say that Zena of the TV fame was a Chica-in-Charge!

Cronehood
Empty nest, the children have left the home and this is what that stage is called in a woman's life.

Cronus pronus
The common-sense age when a woman gives in to the inexorable force of gravity, where wrinkles are character lines, and she starts thinking her mind might be more of an enticement than her figure.

Feminina
A young lady. e.g. "there were many femininas at the beach."

Fluffragette
A woman who has chosen to ignore all the feminist influences in the last few decades and yet draws her heroines from that era.

Frusterbation
When the subject of your affections and lustful desire says no and you are reduced to auto-erotic techniques.

Foreploy
Any advantageous misinterpretation of yourself that benefits your goal of getting laid (males will know exactly what this means)

Genderfriend
A term of neutrality used when one is uncertain of the other's sexuality "Do you have a genderfriend?" "Yes I have a boyfriend"

Gesbian
This is a term to cover both genders of a homosexual persuasion.

Girlcott
Female-only participants of a boycott.

Glibido
A tease, all talk and no action.

Gynoporn
Media that appeals mostly to women's sexual proclivities and not limited to romance or bodice-ripping vignettes but magazines of the more risqué.

Hasbian
Former lesbian, who now dates men. Example: "the most famous hasbian of our time must be Anne Heche."

Heteroflexible
Yes you guessed it, bisexual.

Heterosexist
Attitudes, conditions, or behaviours that promote stereotyping of social roles based on an assumption of heterosexual orientation.

Male co-worker #1: So, I've started seeing someone.
Male co-worker #2: Will I meet them at the company picnic?
Male co-worker #1: Them?!
Male co-worker #2: Well, I didn't want to be heterosexist!

Himbo
A man who is symmetrically good looking, however is also vain and superficial.

Irritable male syndrome
Sudden testosterone levels dropping can cause a man to be tetchy and irritable. May be brought on by stress.

Manny
A man who plays the traditionally female dominated role of nanny.

Manscaping
The skilled trimming and shaping of a man's body hairs.
(Man + landscaping.)

Menglish
Language of the man, about the man and for the man.

Metrosexual
1. A dandyish narcissist in love with not only himself, but also his urban lifestyle. Example: The only problem facing the metrosexual in an otherwise carefree existence is the inescapable effects of ageing. If 30 is 45 in gay years, then 26 is retirement age for the metrosexual, and no amount of biotechnological, rehydrating, whale sperm dermo-care can alter that. 2. An urban male with a strong aesthetic sense who spends a great deal of time and money on his appearance and lifestyle. 3. A male who wants to be gay, but is not; a gay wannabe.

Nagorific
The kind of whine or whinge which is so constant that the person hearing it is able to switch off.

Naggart
A person who nags with some skill.

Petrasexual
Cohort of double-income-no-kids couples who substitute

pets, usually dogs, for children. These pets are subsequently overindulged, pampered and spoilt and given very little obedience training. Owners expect friends to treat these animals as if they were indeed offspring. Visiting petrasexuals will expect their pets to be invited to sit on the furniture, sleep in the family beds, be present throughout meal times and toileted on request—frequently. Holiday and social activities will be limited by the preferences of the pets.

Pregnancy bingo
When you are in the limbo land of not caring whether you do or don't fall pregnant, 'baby roulette'.

Retrosexual
1. A man who refuses to pluck his eyebrows or use hair products. 2. Straight, married, monogamous, faithful parents. 3. A woman who will stay at home, fix dinner, clean the house and take care of the kids. Someone still clinging to the sexual stereotypes of previous era.

Sapiosexuality
When brains act as an aphrodisiac.

Scarlet-collar worker
The madam of a pornographic web site.

Schmoozathon
A couple in a perpetual clinch which seems to go on indefinitely.

Technosexual
Usually a male affliction. The orgasmic delights the man felt about cars and their many intricacies, he now has transferred to technology.

Testosteronic
A male who is stereotypically masculine.

Toxic bachelor
Not exactly good marriage material. He's selfish, insensitive and making no effort to move out of his 'bachelor comfort zone'.

One-uppersonship
The politically correct terminology for one person trying to get ascendancy over another.

Volumptuous
The woman's body which has pleasing curves and gives it a nuance of even more luxurious and generous than voluptuous.

Wife acceptance factor
Where an object which is usually a technical appliance was tailored for men but is being remarketed to appeal to women.

Yestergay
A man who has been a homosexual but is now living as a heterosexual. The female equivalent is a 'hasbian'.

Eat Speak

"I've been on a diet for two weeks
and all I've lost is two weeks".

Totie Fields

Here they are, a smattering of newly coined words that refer to our strange and often dysfunctional approach to eating in the early part of the 21st century.

Ape Diet
The vegetarian's diet whose main source of nutrition derives from ape food, nuts and leafy green vegetables.

Breatharian
Someone who attempts to get all their nutritional needs from the air. At the last count they were an amazingly small minority, and hardly there when turned sideways, but they are leaving a light ecological footprint.

Fatphobic
This is the irrational fear of all things fat and fatty including fat persons who might by association transfer the virus to the phobic if in the same proximate area.

Flexitarian
A non-core vegetarian. One who even though they eat mostly vegetarian they occasionally eat meat and fish too.

Flues
A condition of depression suffered by the weight challenged who are beginning to believe there isn't any way to lose the excess kilos.

Piscetarian
Pisces the zodiac fish sign have, you guessed, this is a vegetarian who now and then supplements their vegetarian fare with fishes.

Orthorexia
This is someone who zealously desires to adhere to eating only healthy foods. On the bible of good nutrition he swears to "eat the good food, only the good food and nothing but the good food".

Deprivation cuisine
1. Ah here we have it! A politically correct euphemism that aptly describes most diets, which more often than not leave you with a list of allowable foods you hate. 2. Food that is healthy and so on but so bland that it isn't that palatable. Why is everything we love bad for us?

Dietsilience
This is the resilience the body demonstrates in the speed with which it regains those pounds in half the time it took the dieter to lose them. It can also mean the speed with which said dieter goes from being a fad diet devotee to being the biggest critic "Well I did everything it said but it didn't work for me".

Diet Fatigue
There comes a time in a serial dieter's life when they finally throw up their hands in exasperation and say "I'm sick of all this! The only thing that's stayed off is the money I spent on all these programs" No offers in these fat loss schemes of "Get your money back if you've gained the weight again within the next six months".

Diabesity
Obesity + diabetes. The double whammy, this is diabetes caused by excess weight.

Nyr-dietism
This is the worldwide phenomenon practised by the overweight and not so overweight in the weeks after the New Year when excessive food consumption has been practiced by most western consumers. "New Year's resolution" diet.

Globesity
Hot on the heels of globalisation comes globesity, which signifies the worldwide epidemic of obesity.

Obesogenic
Of or relating to causes or factors which tend to cause obesity: genetics, food consumption a couple that spring to mind.

Passive Overeating
Because the body is slow to recognise the caloric content of rich foods, there is an inclination to eat excesses of foods high in fat; if you are someone who eats all that is put in front of you even to the point of discomfort you are a victim of passive overeating. To be fair though, this is much like the airborne toxins we breathe every day and are unaware of them because of their invisibility. If foods could throw up warnings like the little prompts on our computer screens "Are you sure you want to consume this? It is 10,000 calories which is your caloric quota for an entire week" Another meaning for passive overeating is to explain the phenomenon of the person who claims "Oh I only have to window shop at the patisserie and I can feel the pounds going on!"

Stealth Fat
This is the covert fat, the fat equivalent to the CIA. Known officially as trans fatty acids or trans fats, that don't have to proclaim their presence on the ingredients label in foods. What chance do we stand with these fattist guerillas lying in wait to ambush our diet resolutions? (It's also called phantom fat)

Sliminazi
This is a woman mostly who, like the born again non-smoker, wastes no conversational opportunity to tell anyone and everyone what a wonderful person they are now that they are adhering to the "diet". A blow-by-blow account of all the little moments and insights of being lighter and more in control of their eating. They

are fascistitic by virtue of the barely veiled "Ye less than perfect fat people, why can't you be as strong-willed and virtuous as I am?"

Rawist
Someone who eats only unprocessed, unheated and uncooked food, especially organic fruits, nuts, grains and vegetables. Raw meat, even if you weren't a vegetarian would be an unpalatable option, you would imagine.

Salad Dodger
Someone who shuns healthy food and may as a result be overweight although this does not apply to the nomads who live on the plains of Mongolia and eat no vegetables but nevertheless remain quite lean. "If it's green then don't put it on my plate, if it grew in the ground don't bother either. My options are further up the food chain".

Diet Cop
Official and unofficial. These are the persons who monitor another person's weight loss program. So they can be a weight loss counsellor, Jenny Craig for example or your mum or a friend who seems to take nearly more of an interest in the progress than you do.

Gastronaut
To go where no other eater has gone before you.
The adventurous eater.

Slow food
This is a gastronomical movement who are up in arms about the steady creep of 'fast food' and emphasise traditional organic growing methods and the appreciation of fine food and wine and the fast disappearing art of sitting at a table and sharing a congenial meal with friends or family instead of the "getting something on the run" relay that's played out in many a domicile these days.

Fast-casual
A cut above the fast food franchise. Not quite a fast food, not quite a restaurant in the sense that you don't have to wait until they kill and cure the meat before being served.

Eater-tainment
The holistic approach to the eating experience where mounted memorabilia are on display, video feeds or live music to make it all more palatable.

Drive-through cuisine
Drive in, talk to the box, give your order, "I'll have a double whopper zinger burger, quarter pounder deluxe with cheese and bacon, hold the pickles, with a pepsi". "Will that be all, will you have fries with that?" Go around to the first window and pay up as they pass you your 'fast food' at any number of outlets.

Deskfast
Breakfast eaten at your desk usually in the morning. Can lead to a strange assortment of food residue landing on keyboard.

Wakefast
The meal that is eaten upon waking up, between noon and 3:00 p.m. that is both a (late) lunch and the first meal of the day. (In contrast with brunch, which somehow involves grapefruit.) Example: "On Saturday I rolled out of bed somewhere around 2:30 and had a hearty wakefast of Ramen noodles and cheddar cheese combos."

Dashboard dining
Some who knows they will be caught in a snarl of traffic on their way to work, choose to have their breakfast a la dash. Some even do their toilette inside their vehicles—faces get shaved, makeup applied, teeth brushed and flossed.

Cup-holder cuisine
Food designed to be placed in a cup holder that is consumed in a car or a truck.

Exercise bulimia
Compulsive behaviour where a person calculates the caloric content of the meal they're consuming and then designs a workout which will burn off the exact number of calories. "Sorry can't make it tonight—having eaten a profiterole at afternoon tea I now have to do 3 hours on my Steperciser tonight."

Chairobics
Aerobics whilst sitting in a chair or a wheelchair. Why stand when you can sit?

Urban Yoga
Another name for Yogacise. Where the traditional yoga stretches team up with high impact aerobics set to music. Sounds oxymoronic I know but it's out there and quite popular.

Korporatese

"I am amazed at how eager the CEOs of the biggest companies are today to communicate as effectively as possible, to employ the skills and the language."

Frank Lutz

Here in contrast are words coined to describe better and explain the reality of work life in the early 21st century. Can you relate to any of these?

Adhocracy
Here's an organisation with little formal structure which operates by ad hoc teams and cross functional groups, it's either a great success or sheer chaos!

Administrivia
It's all those odds and ends on a website that just don't fit anywhere else, not even under miscellaneous, copyright, disclaimers or legalese.

Alpha pup
A term used for Mr Cool-the-Midas-of-the-business-world. "We'll see if the alpha pup goes for the idea, and if he does we're bound to make gazillions."

Anonymise
One of the growing-"ise" family. They take an adjective and turn into into a verb in this case "to make anonymous".

Barcode rape
When you're at an Expo or some such and the "booth bunnies" grab your nametag and swipe it even before they've started the hard sell. You feel violated.

Blamestorming
A group exercise done with the benefit of hindsight to try to apportion blame for failed venture on anyone but themselves.

Blix
An eponym, named after Dr Hans Blix, one of the UN weapons inspectors who found no weapons of mass destruction. "We blixed it and found nothing."

Bobbleheading
Like sunflowers nodding in the breeze, it's the collective action of the heads around the table bobbing up and down in abject agreement with their superior.

Bohica
An acronym that the real workers mutter under their breath when the managers announce their latest sales/customer service/quality initiative, Bend Over, Here It Comes Again.

Botchulism
Bandaid and shortcut solutions in business which turn toxic "Rob Deakin's last initiative gave the company a bad case of botchulism".

Brown bag session
When you're required to attend a lunchtime meeting which is not catered for. Bring your own lunch.

Chimping
The "Oooh, hhooo! Ooo!" made by digital camera enthusiasts when they spot a good shot on their feedback screen.

Circling the drain
What a company does just before it's about to sink below the surface, just like dirty bath water as it makes its way down the plug hole.

Coma factor
The measure used for the dullness and sleep makingness of a meeting or presentation. "Let's try to get through this afternoon with as low a coma factor as possible."

Corbesity
Corporate obesity. When a company has become fat and lazy and isn't trying to stay on the cutting edge any more. Time to trim the fat!

Corporate anorexia
When the company has taken its fat trimming too far. Instead of making the organization healthy it often leads to bankruptcy and the death spiral.

Corridor warriors
Those poor itinerant execs and employees who spend their whole day rushing from one meeting to another and quickly utilizing laptops in between to take notes and keep up with emails coming in.

Cubicle vultures
When a worker has been laid off or fired, his work mates hang around the abandoned cubicle and strip it bare of anything that moves: swivel chairs, desk lamps, credenzas and so on.

Cyberslackers
Employees who use the company's internet to play games, check their personal email, stock options, humour sites.

Death-by-bullet-pointlessness
The inclination for managers to use the medium of Powerpoint and to use "enhance, facilitate, implement" at the beginning of every bullet, until the audience struggles to keep from going into a coma.

Deja moo
That niggling feeling that you might have heard this bull before.

Director of First Impressions
The receptionist who meets and greets. What started out as a bit of a spoof has finished up being a real job title in some companies!

Dispense suspense
Those few microseconds between making a selection on the self-serve machine when there is complete silence and then suddenly it whirrs into action and pops out what you ordered.

Document polish
These are the fancy phrases and buzzwords added to a presentation to give it the window dressing, but add no appreciable value.

Drive-by download
One of those insidious sites that downloads onto your computer automatically often without your consent.

Dub-dub-dub
Short for www. It's used often by technicians when they're giving the URL details on sites they are tinkering with.

Duck shuffler
Just when you've managed to get all those "ducks in a row" the duck shuffler, often a manager, stuffs it up and you have to go back to the drawing board.

E-dundant
An annoying habit the middle managers have of following up a subordinates email with their own, more than likely trying to steal the credit.

Empty suit
Here's a term for an executive who lacks the skills, talents, experience, nous and intellect to justify being in that position.

Evergreening,
This is the process of keeping your web page content current, up to date and relevant.

Eye chart
This is when someone is using a PowerPoint presentation and has crammed a lot of information on just the one slide making it very hard to read.

Faith-based intelligence
Here's a top down approach to management. They say "We have the answers, now you supply the detail to support them".

Faulty-tasking
When multi-tasking ends up with a few juggled eggs smashed on the ground.

Ghost work
One of their colleagues is laid off and this is what the others pick up to keep the show on the road, often with little or no recognition from management—sometimes these jobs are not filled for months.

Hamsterise
This is what companies do with some work, they use manual labour, el cheapo hamsters instead of technology.

Heat-seeking workforce
The group of workers who move to a company when it's strong on the share market but who move off once the share price drops.

Homing from work
The use of latest technologies, cell phone, SMS, IM and so on to keep in touch with the family. Once frowned upon as doing "personal business on company time", it's now encouraged so employees don't feel guilty about working late.

Hoovering
This is the fine art of sucking up.

Hot desking or Location independent working
Is the term used for works who have no permanent workstation and are given temporary workspace to fit the task. In other words having no where to hang your hat, being homeless.

Idiotoxic
This is found in political campaigns, courts of law and government regulations. It's an idea, concept or activity which is detrimental to

the health of the organization, if not the nation.

Integrity Deficit Disorder
This is a politically correct term for a person who has trouble differentiating between honesty and deceit.

Keepage
A quaint antonym to "garbage".

Krudzu
Any fast growing management fad or other hair brained scheme which takes over and eventually strangles an organization much as a strangler fig does away with its host tree.

Malicious obedience
Where the employees go through the motions of doing their work whilst accomplishing nothing in protest to something the organization has once again thrust upon them.

Management insultancy
This is when the management employ a consultancy to formulate what they should be doing, finding the best ways to run the company.

Meeting moth:
An executive so bent on flitting from meeting to meeting but seldom actioning anything.

New guy gene
The initial veneer that a new employee wears until they become savvy about office politics. Being nice and obsequious and helpful to everyone, no job too hard etc.

Passing the trash
When an employee is passed on to another department or organization without pointing out that person's shortcomings with regard to work.

Percussive maintenance
The time honoured practice which used to be applied to vending machines is now being employed on minor equipment such as Xerox machines, fax machines and hard drives. Whack it and watch it whirr into life!

PowerPointless
1. The "oh no not another PowerPoint presentation! Not Bullet Points!" Effect. 2. Within in a PowerPoint presentation, the bells and whistles offered by the program that add no value whatsoever.

Scooby snacks
The company's token compensation for good works. Usually non-monetary and non-significant and usually regarded with disdain by the employees.

Sheeple
Companies turning employees and consumers into herd animals which follow blindly are called "sheeple".

Sidewalk meeting
The real stuff happens when managers are grabbing a quick fag break outside the building, making plans and coalitions with other co-smokers of course!

Silver ceiling
The glass ceiling is for women, the silver for older workers who find it very difficult to advance in the organization because of the bias to the younger gun.

Six-inch calibration
Akin to "percussive maintenance" but it involves raising the piece of technology slightly off the surface and dropping it in the hopes of making the blessed thing work!

Slaptops
"Desk rage" is on the rise, the chief reason for frustration levels being non compliant technology. Thus PCs are being recoined as "slaptops".

Sloptions
Stock options which aren't worth feeding to the hens or the goldfish. Even though these were a feature of the dot.com revolution, it has become apparent that they've been around for years.

Smogging
This is a sales term where the salesman does such a hyped up pitch that there is no way the product can live up to expectations.

Soddi Defence
Some Other Dude Did It. In law, the defence team that makes an argument that there were any other numbers of individuals who could have done the crime with which their client is being charged.

So 15 minutes ago
"that concept is so 15 minutes ago", in others is past its use by date.

Slacktivism
A form of activism be it social, political or environmental, which happens from the safety of the computer terminal.

Success virus
When the win-win turns a company into an accelerated series of successes due to the morale boosting effect of being a winner.

Sudden Reputation Death Syndrome
Only the top execs suffer from this malady. It occurs when a stumble or mistake is discovered and leads to a downward spiral leading to loss of job and reputation.

The 10,000-foot view
This is another term for the "big picture" or the overview. Further exaggerations such as the "33 thousand-foot view" have also been seen.

Tick-tock
"We're trying to stay focused on the big picture, not the tick-tock." Also this term is used when the press go to the limit recounting the dramatic moment by moment details of an event.

Up-titling
This describes the tendency of organizations to give impressive sounding titles to jobs instead of raises in salary. The Head of Verbal Telecommunications is really a receptionist. An Optical Illuminator Enhancer cleans windows. And Stock Replenishment Executives stock shelves. In other words, fussy window dressing that fools no one.

Viral marketing
Not to be confused with a bad chain letter, this is email's answer to "word of mouth". One person emails 10 friends who email 10 friends and so on until the whole world beats a path to your door.

Warm-chair attrition
Another term for "presenteeism", where an unhappy worker stops giving it his all and only ends when they leave the organization to find another job.

Word-of-mouse
The Net way of spreading things. Just think of how many sites you see the "tell a friend" button .

Work spasm
This is the exceptionally energized working spurt someone coming off their vacation or a relaxing weekend suffers from. It usually wears off half way through their first day back.

Baby Boomer Speak

Times are changing. Government talks of the "ageless employee", people continuing to work beyond retirement age. Maybe because they won't be able to afford to retire.

Also with regard to work/life balance, because people are living longer, there is more need for leave to be taken not only for the care of children but for the older relatives.

And the baby boomers who are now getting into their sixties will and are changing the face of what it means to age. The expectation is that they will stay active far beyond the parameters of generations of yore.

Here are some of the new terms to cope with the phenomenon:

Age defiant
A whole generation of people, the baby boomers. They say now that today's 70s are yesterdays 50s. They are re-inventing the senior years. Not a time to sit on the porch, rocking slowly and reminiscing about the good old days, not a time for donning the slippers and getting a walking stick. No this generation believe that age is only a number, they are looking towards the future and viewing the Third Age as the best time of their lives, to learn, to travel, to be free of family responsibilities, to be relatively healthy, to become active socially, politically and environmentally.

Active aging
A break from the past, where people remain active mentally and physically for much longer.

Adultescent
A middle aged person who goes on enjoying the culture of youth.

Andrologist
A doctor who specialises in men's health, especially the health of the male reproductive system.

Andropause
Man's counterpart to menopause when changes occur due to the drop in testosterone.

Boomeritis
The baby boomers who are still involved in athletics and sport on an amateur basis but are carrying injuries.

Botox party
A gathering where the party goers are botoxed by a doctor who is specifically there to give them the wrinkle defying treatment.

Communal bereavement
A typical incident of this was the communal reaction to Princess Di's demise, or else after the Bali incident or post tsunami. It's collective grieving for people not known personally to us.

Cremains
The remains of someone who's been cremated.

Criminal menopause
When a criminal no longer has the taste for the crimes he committed in his heyday, he is going through criminal menopause and is no longer a danger to society.

Cronehood
The children have finally left home and the woman can be said to be entering her cronehood.

Death care industry
The burgeoning industry based around funeral homes, prepaid funerals and the like.

Elder
A verb meaning to mentor and counsel those younger than oneself

Elder orphan
When your family can't or won't take care of you in your old age you are said to be an "elder orphan".

Elderweds
Yes the grey counterpart to newlyweds. More people are getting married well into the third age.

Eternity leave
This is paid leave given to someone who must care full time for a dying parent or partner.

Geezer glut
The influx of seniors who will form part of the seniors brigade. The baby boomers are living longer and are more demanding than past generations.

Grandboomer
If you're a grandparent and part of the baby boomers, you're a grandboomer.

Granny leave
Flexible or reduced working hours afforded to someone who is the carer for an elderly relative.

Grey matter
Older, experienced executives hired by start-up firms in an effort to make the firms appear more established.

Grey nomad
At any time in Australia you have the retiree travellers who spend a good bit of their time touring in their recreational vehicles and campervans.

Grief tourist
The people who visited the tsunami swept countries or went to Bali after the bombing are said to be "grief tourists".

Kidult
An older person in touch with their inner child, still enjoying youth culture.

Leather spinster
A woman who is heterosexual or asexual and happily single with no wish to find a mate.

Makeunder
The antidote to makeover it's a playing down of makeup and a simpler hairstyle, like a seachange for appearance.

Memory glasses
This is a memory aid to the likes of Alzheimer's sufferers. The small video camera is attached to the glasses and has access to the computer which prompts the wearer as to the familiar faces and things and their names.

Memory prosthesis
A device that helps a person remember things such as the glasses just described.

Menopot
The middle aged spread experienced sometimes by post menopausal women.

Middlescence
The turbulent, rebellious middle age of the baby boom generation.

Middle youth
The late 20s to early 40s where the person is no longer considered young and not old or middle aged and is having a hard time facing the prospect of middle age.

Neanimorphic
Someone who looks younger than they are.

Norc
Naturally Occurring Retirement Community; it's a block of flats or a neighbourhood where most of the residents have grown old.

Perma-youth
Someone who uses the aid of cosmetic surgery to keep a youthful appearance.

Post-mortem divorce
This is an agreement where one specifies that one does not want to be interred with one's ex-partner

Protirement
Quitting or retiring an unattractive job to pursue hobbies or a lifestyle much more suitable to one's personality.

Quarterlife crisis
Crisis of confidence usually in mid to late twenties post education about what to do for the rest of their lives.

Retirement panic
When retirement is looming and a person suddenly feels anxiety and panic about maybe not being able to live in retirement.

Retrogenesis
The unravelling of memory and personality which is in reverse order to the way we gained these in childhood.

Seachanger
A person who makes a decision to downsize the hours and the pressure from their job, often moving either to the seaside or the country. Stopping to smell the roses or the seaweed.

Senior moment
A momentary lapse in memory, particularly one experienced by a senior citizen.

Silver ceiling
The grey equivalent to the woman's glass ceiling. The prejudice against older employees making it difficult for them to advance in an organization.

Six down
A crossword enthusiast who has passed away.

Skipped generation
Where the grandparents are the sole care givers to the grandchildren.

Yoghurt cities
This is the answer to the baby boomers moving on from retirement communities. There will be cities with thriving "active cultures", opera, museums, sporting facilities, bookstores, etc.

"A honey tongue, a heart of gall."

Portuguese proverb

"A lie will go around the world,
while truth is pulling its boots on."

Proverb

"The limits of my language mean the limits of my world."

Ludwig Wittgenstein 1921,
Tractatus Logico Philosophicus